Art and Faith

mixed media art
with a faith-filled message

Cherie Burbach

cherieburbach.com

Art and Faith

Bonjour
Publishing

Copyright © 2016 by Cherie Burbach

ISBN 978-0-9972274-0-6

ART AND FAITH

mixed media art with a faith-filled message

Cover and interior art by Cherie Burbach

Printed in the United States of America

Art

and

Faith

Also by Cherie Burbach

Nonfiction

100 Simple Ways to Have More Friends

5 Weeks to Form a New Friendship

Glass Sculptures: How to Make Beautiful Sculptures for the Garden Using Vases, Bowls, and Other Glass Pieces

Emotional Affairs: How to Prevent, Stop, and Move On From an Emotional Affair

How to (Really) Make Money Blogging

21 Simple Things You Can Do To Help Someone With Diabetes

Internet Dating Is Not Like Ordering a Pizza

21 Ways to Promote Your Book on Twitter

Creative Planner: Perpetual Day Planner for Creative People

Poetry

Angel Toughness

My Soul Is From a Different Place

Father's Eyes

The Difference Now

A New Dish

New and Selected Poems

Yes, You

Reviews for Cherie Burbach's Poetry

"There is so much depth to these poems.
Even if you don't typically read poetry,
this book will speak to your heart!"

"The faith and hope that echo in her poems
will connect well with readers."

"This was a very nice collection of poetry
that I was really happy to find at this time in my life.
Its connection to God shows through in every word
and the thoughtful themes examined have really moved me."

Cherie Burbach

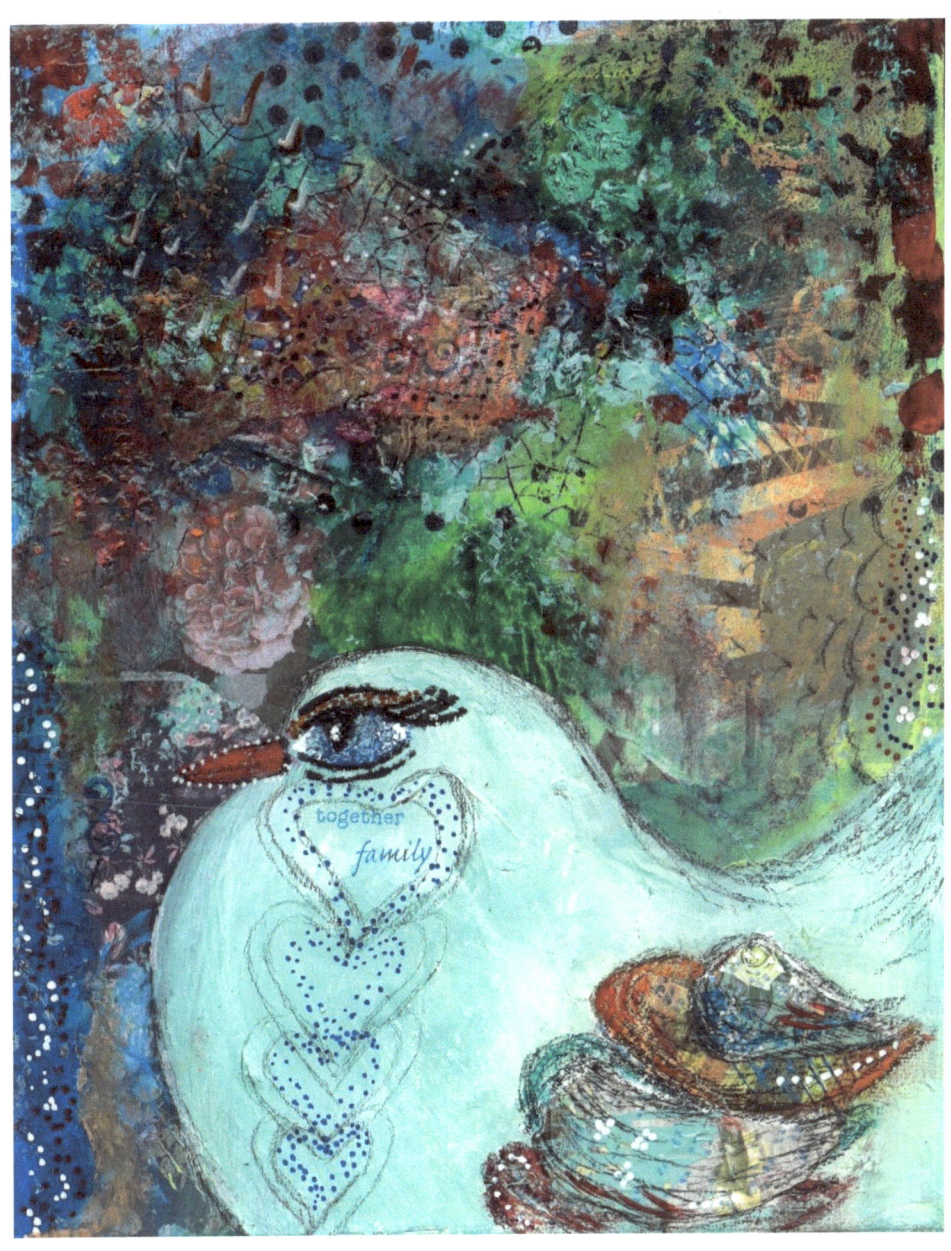

Cherie Burbach

Contents

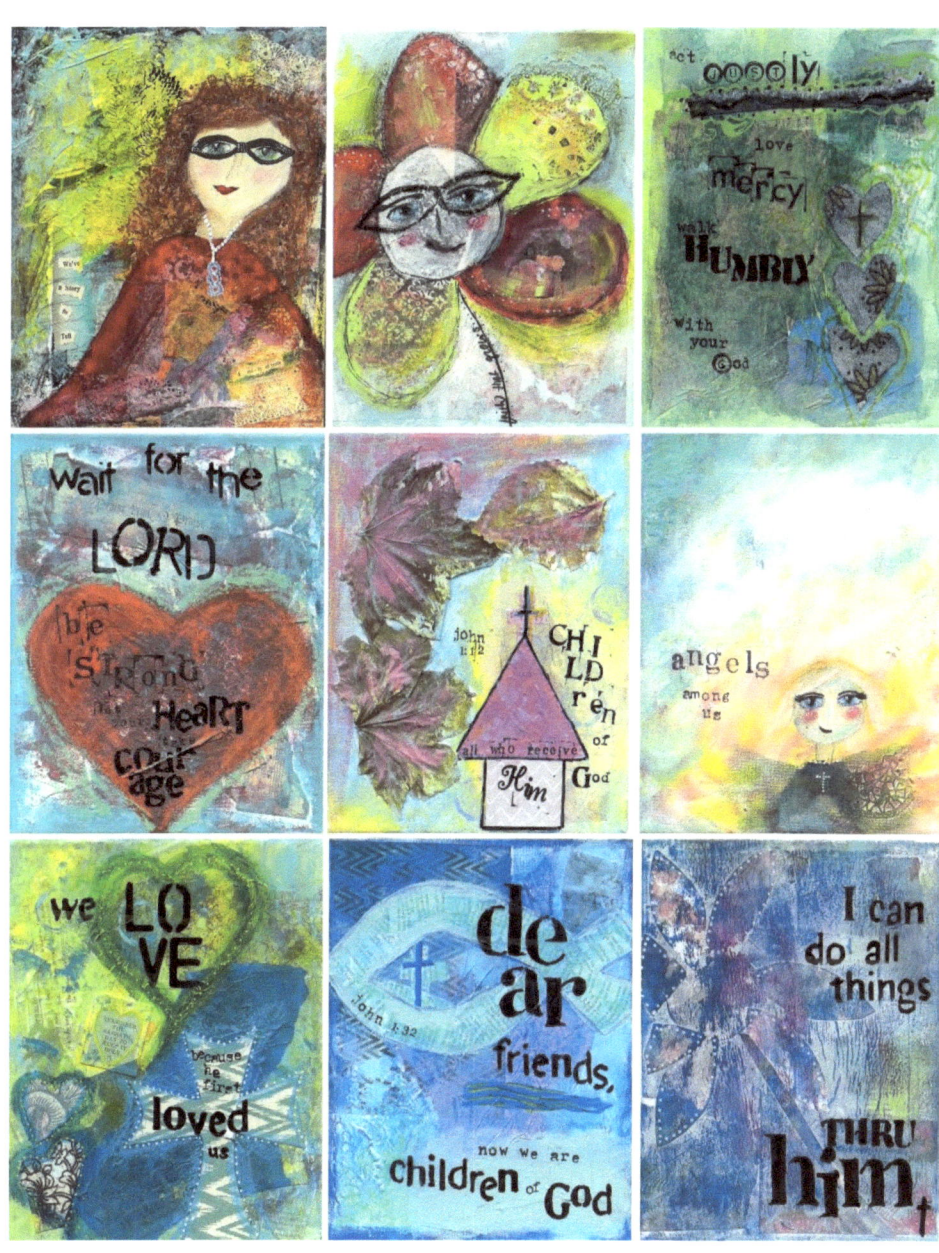

Cherie Burbach

Introduction

Art has always been a creative outlet for me. As far back as I can remember, I illustrated stories from my imagination with crayons and then watercolors, and finally, oils and acrylics. I experimented with inks and different paints and liked the way each type of pigment changed a painting. For years I focused on acrylics simply for the ease of use. They were convenient to keep in my apartment when I felt like painting, and clean up was a breeze.

I painted for years as a way to express myself or just shake off the stresses of the day. Painting was a hobby for me then, separate from my job writing for companies and magazines. That changed in 2004 when I painted a cover for my first book, *The Difference Now*. That book had tremendous meaning for me because it represented a marked change in how I approached (what my aunt calls) my creative gifts. I always wrote stories and poems since I was very young, but I came from a rough background, with an alcoholic father who criticized everything I did. His verbal abuse caused me to be self-conscious of anything I did, including my writing and painting. As a result, I would

> My art time became a kind of prayer time for me.

destroy my stories and poems soon after I'd complete them. Publishing my first book was something I did just for me, a way to prove something to myself.

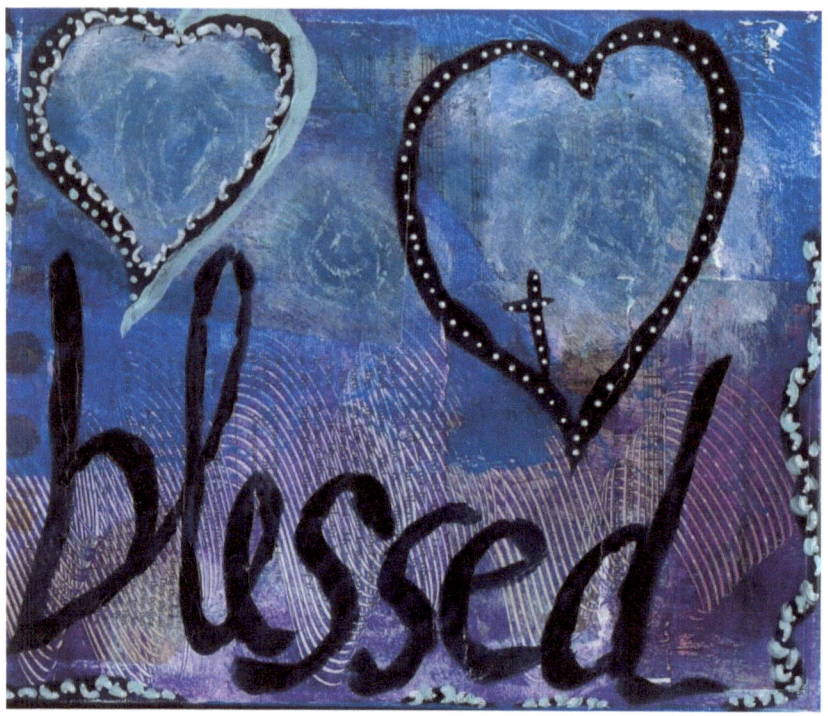

The great news is that the book was well-received, and it gave me confidence to continue writing. I went on to publish six more poetry books, painting the covers of each of them. Painting remained an integral part of my life as a creative entrepreneur, and a few years ago I made the connection between my love of words with my love of art when I discovered mixed media. I felt truly alive as an artist, as if my soul had opened up to God in a whole new way. I enjoyed building the layers, making creative choices on where to paste special papers and layer colors, and which types of paints and applications would work for my pictures.

Cherie Burbach

In choosing the subjects for my paintings, I found myself drawn to God's word in a new way. Although I'd read many of the same passages over and over I was inspired by the images they called up in my mind. As I painted I pondered the message in each verse and felt closer to God as I created. My art time became a kind of prayer time for me.

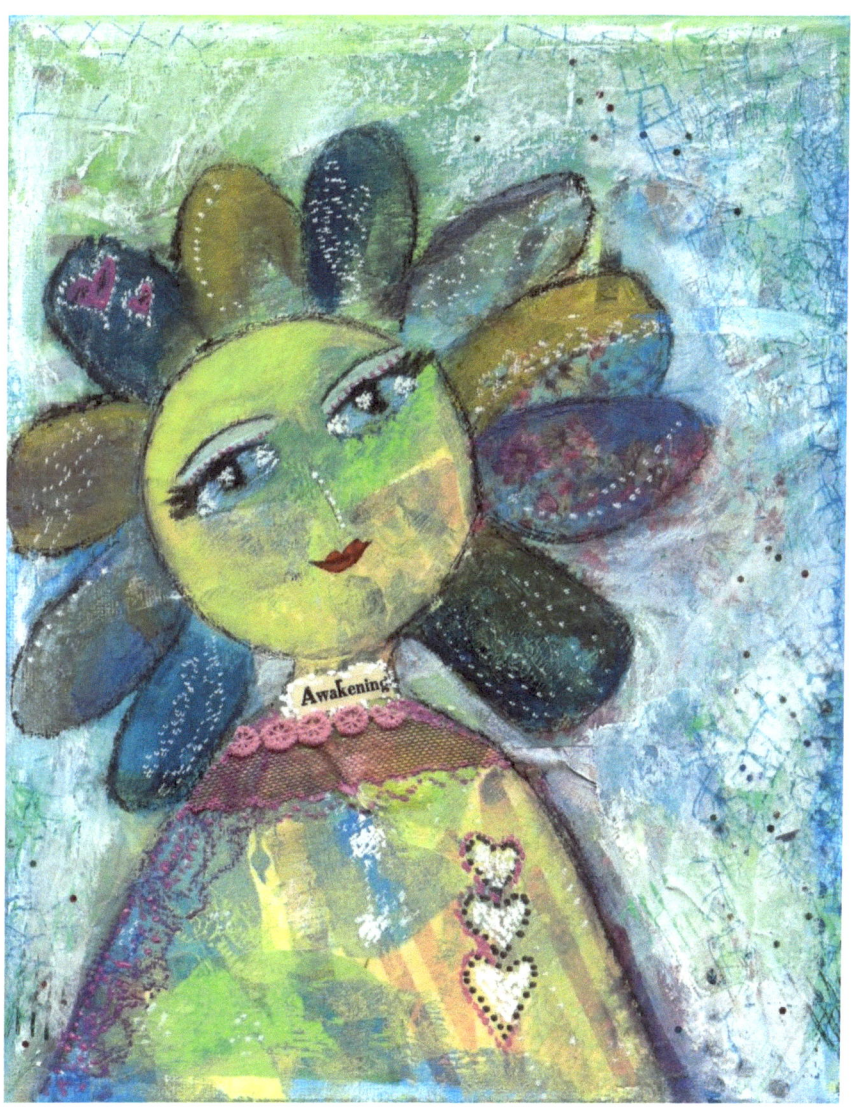

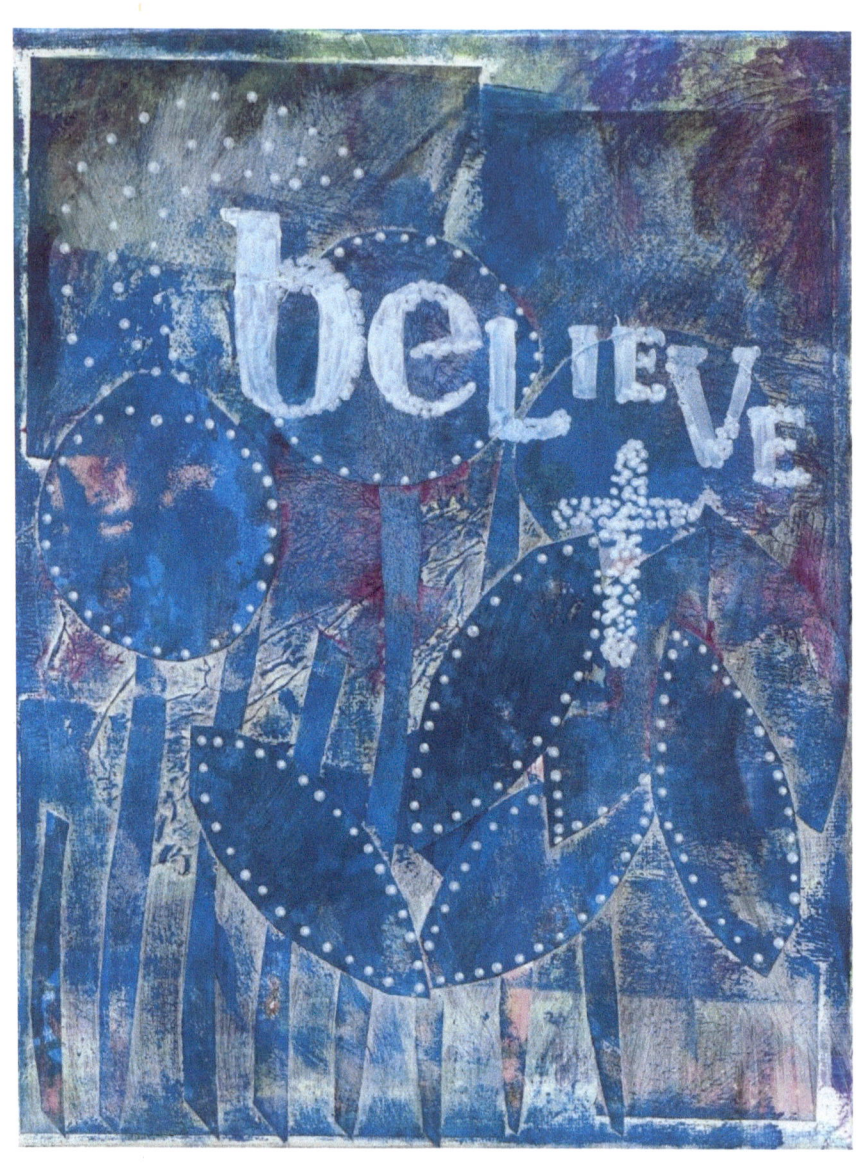

Cherie Burbach

My Faith Story

When I was about three, I begged my mom to go to Sunday School. I was far too young, but she called a local church and was able to get me in. I was so excited, learning about Jesus. She said the first day I came home thrilled to learn that Jesus' mother's name was Mary.

This hunger started in me so young that I don't remember a time in my life where I didn't have God in my heart. I am so thankful for that, especially as I look back on things. I had a rough childhood, which caused me to have a rough early adulthood, and without God, I'm not sure where I would have been. He's helped me through everything, leading me, giving me a strong spirit and a love that is unending. Infinitely patient, He's continued to teach me every day of my life.

> You don't need to settle for anything less than the life God intended for you.

For many years I've written about my background because so many of you have had similar experiences. An abusive, alcoholic parent, lots of lies, lots of being told you weren't good enough from even before you could walk. I've heard from many of you who have told me about your childhood, and how it has affected your adulthood. I write about my childhood because I want you to know there is a way out of that ugly world of addiction and abuse. I write because those painful years are behind me, and God has given me a path to find happiness, have a balanced view of myself, and have solid, loving relationships.

You don't need to settle for anything less than the life God intended for you. Now, don't get me wrong, things are aren't always easy. Life is work. But you can work on being happy, or work on being miserable. Which would you rather do?

> I like to paint about themes that have inspired me in the hopes that they will inspire you, too.

I've shared my story to tell you that I am not perfect, but God has been patient with me. He's pulled me out of darkness and given me a whole new world. He can do this with you, too. Trust that you deserve and are worthy of love. Then, open up your heart to God and let Him show you the path to take.

God blessed me with a love of words and of color and art. In the last few years, I've fallen in love with mixed media painting. I like combining special papers with Bible quotes and a variety of paints and inks to create my art, and I find the process so freeing and forgiving.

As far as the verses I choose for my art, they vary greatly. Sometimes I'm reading a verse that just stands out to me in a way it didn't before. There are times when I read certain passages because I'm looking for inspiration or answers, and other times

Cherie Burbach

where certain words just seem to pop out at me. I think God gives us a nudge when He wants us to really pay attention to a particular message, and this can happen when a verse you've read many times before suddenly becomes clearer to you or seems to take on new meaning.

I also pay attention to the types of verses people ask me about as they visit my booth at craft fairs or write to me. There are favorite verses that people like to see, and I'm always interested in learning about the specific words that mean the most to them. (To *you*!)

We're lucky that we also have so many different versions of the Bible, from the traditional King James Version (KJV) to the New International Version (NIV). I go back and forth between these versions quite heavily depending on the verse, and occasionally I might even use the English Standard Version (ESV).

I like to paint about themes that have inspired me in the hopes that they will inspire you, too. I get letters from people each week who have read my articles or poetry or enjoyed my artwork. What a sweet blessing it is to hear from you like that. But know this, that if something I write or paint helps you grow and moves you, it's all because of God.

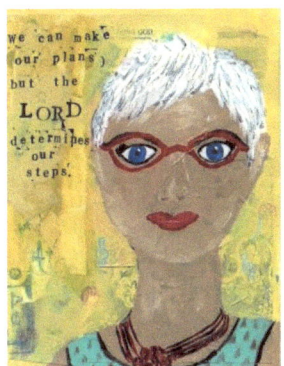 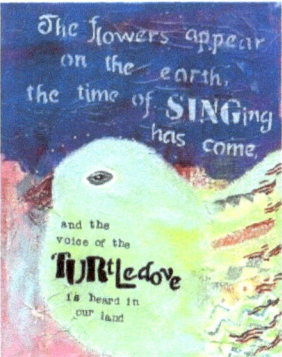 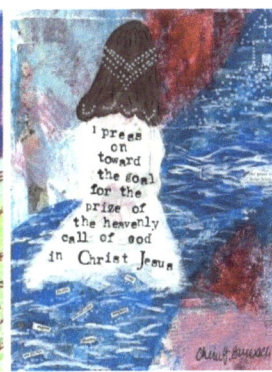

Paintings and Verses

The verses that stood out to me the most in the beginning are the ones I share on the following pages. I always find it amazing how a verse you've read over and over during the years suddenly has new meaning to you. Or, when you're struggling with a certain issue, how a single word or passage will seem to jump off the page and catch your attention.

That's the process I used to choose these verses and create these paintings. Very often there was something in the verse that stood out to me. When I go to craft fairs I am often asked if I have pictures with certain verses on them, and I take note of these as well. Many of us have a favorite verse we go to, almost as a theme for our life.

> I always find it amazing how a verse you've read over and over during the years suddenly has new meaning to you.

Cherie Burbach

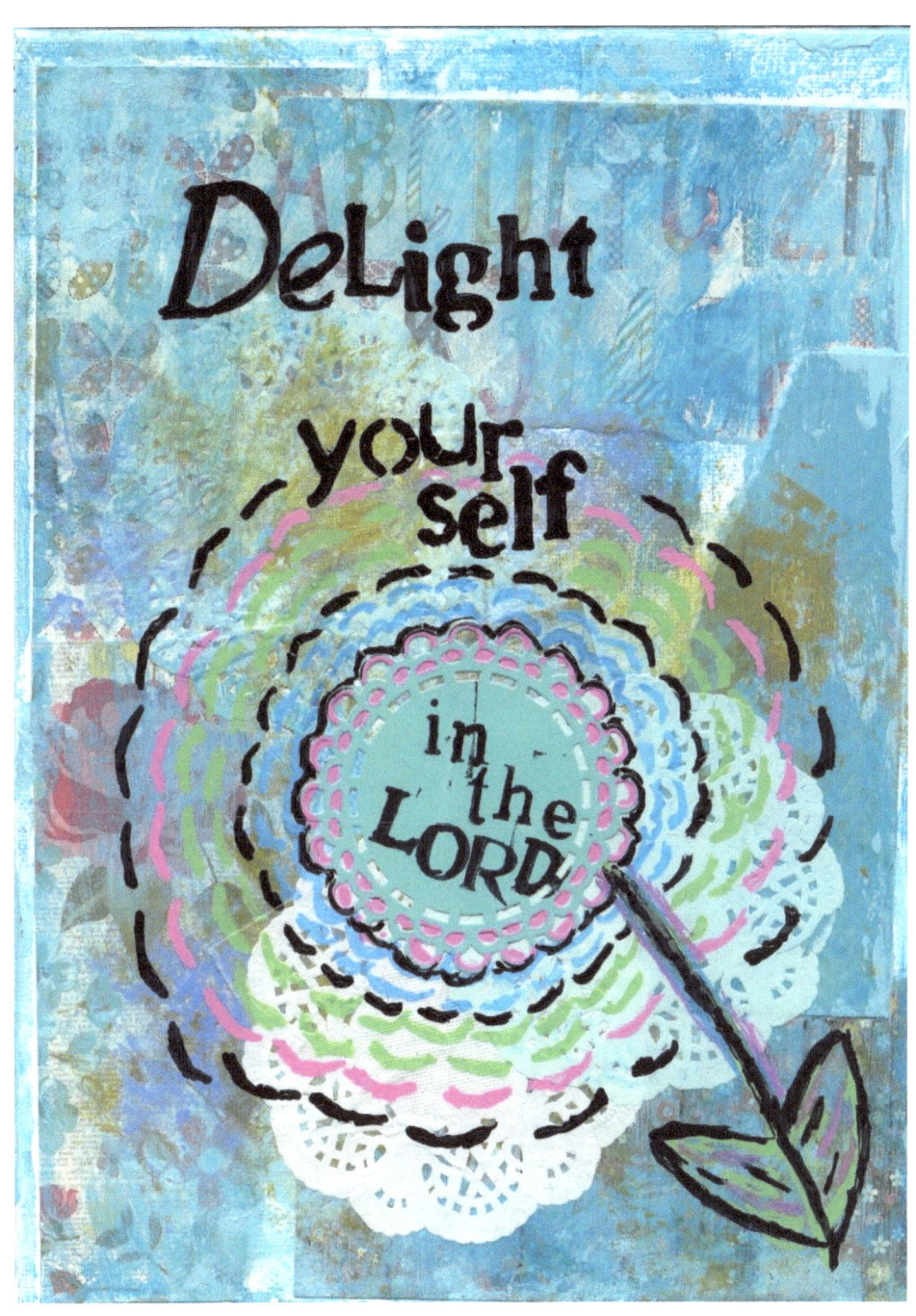

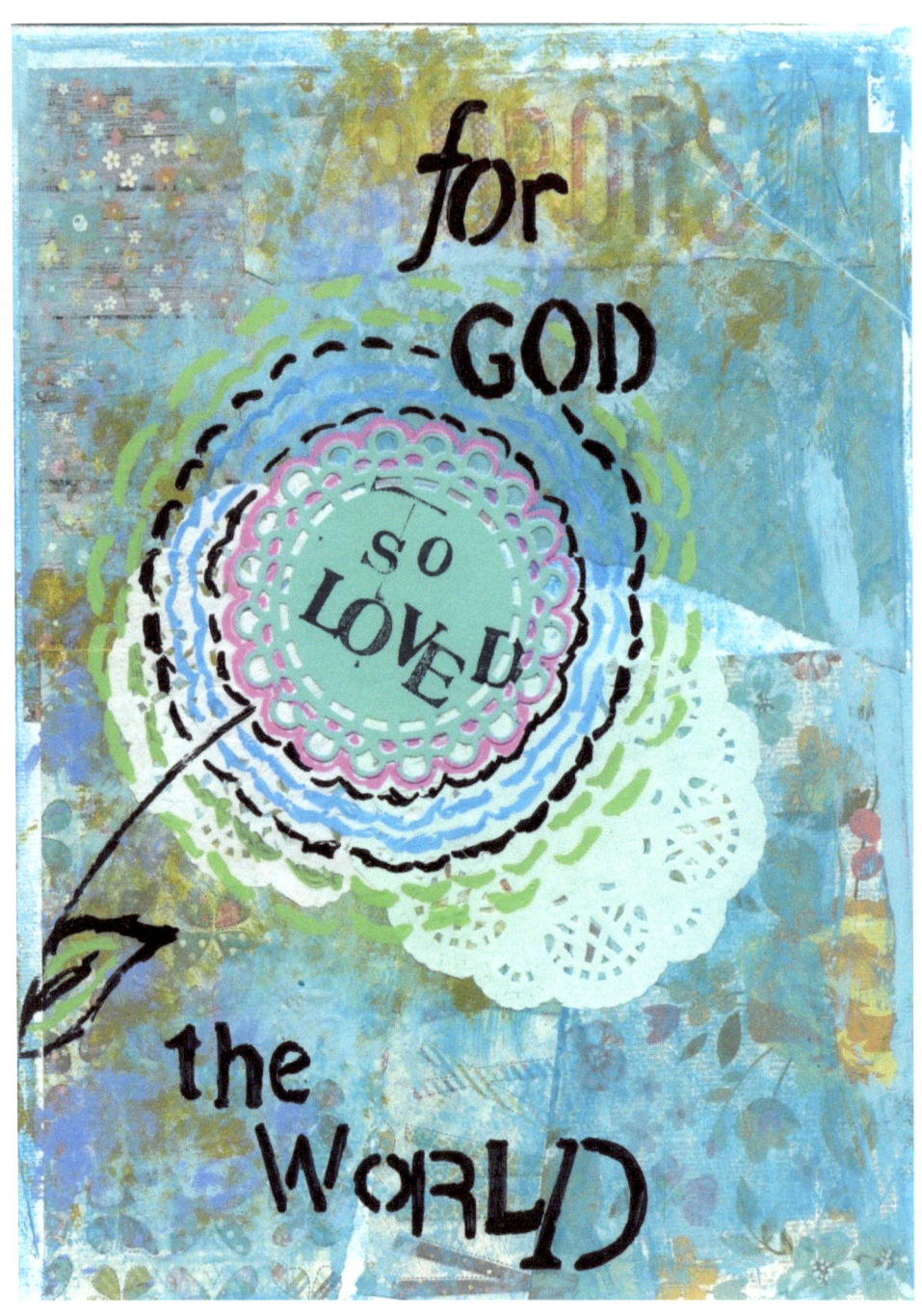

Cherie Burbach

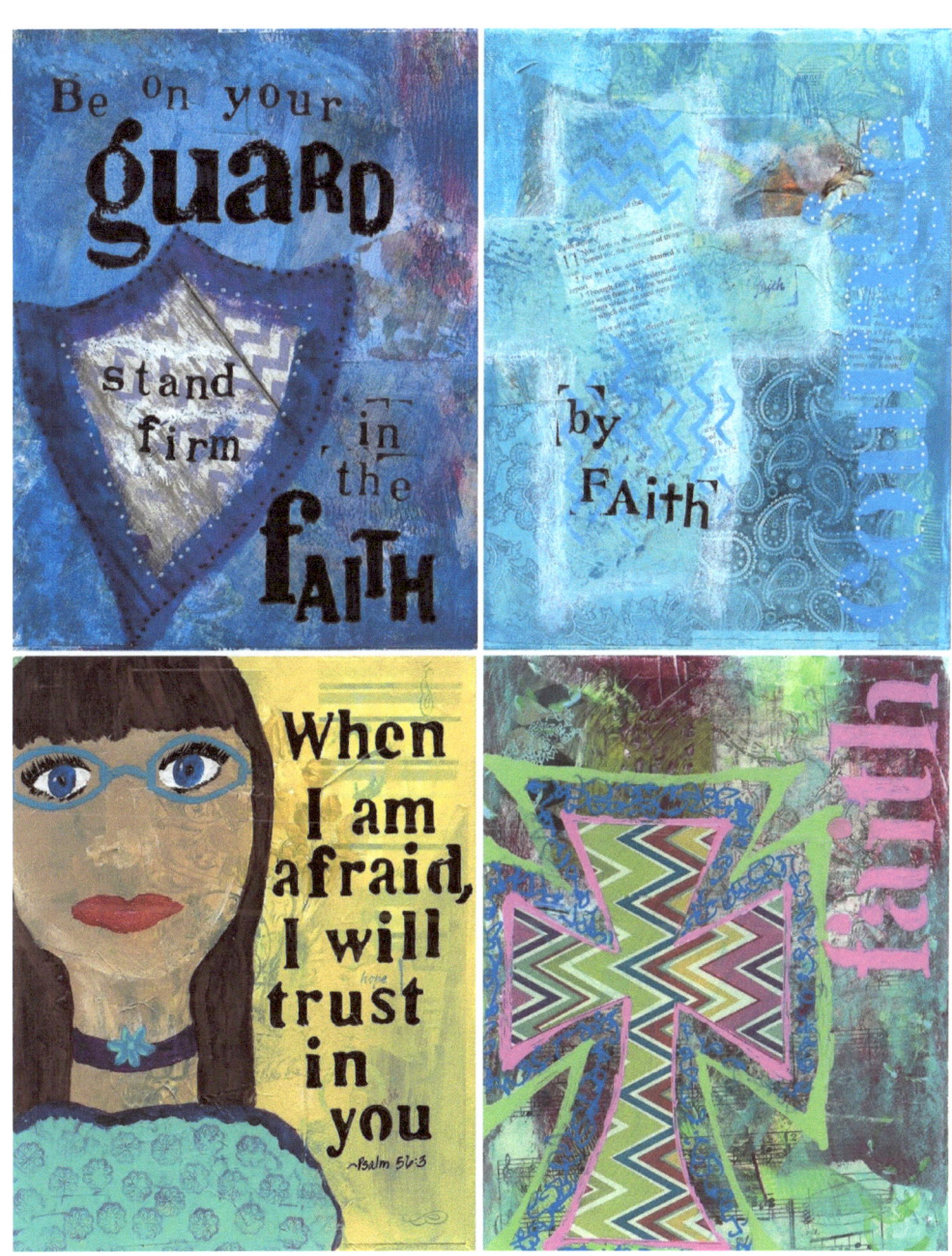

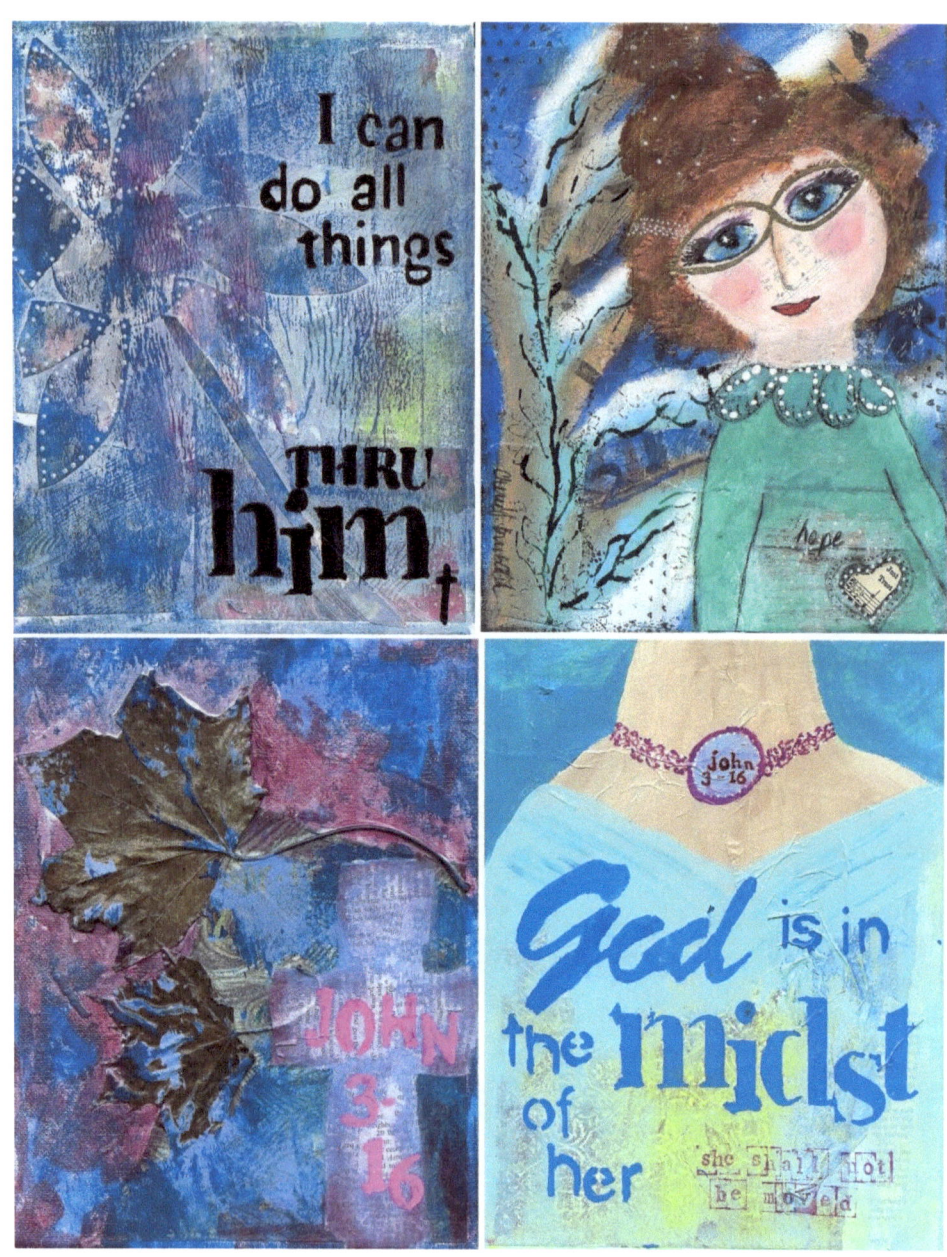

Cherie Burbach

Flawless, Safe in Your Refuge, and You Make My Lot Secure

I enjoy doing a series of pictures that are centered on a specific theme or color scheme. Very often complimentary verses from different parts of the Bible help to make a certain message stand out, and I enjoy combining these into the pictures I create.

For these three paintings, I chose verses that represented security and feeling safe with God on our side. I used a variety of papers, music sheets, doilies, and paint for this series, and painted free form crosses that stood out against a blue background. The verse number for these passages is stamped in blue on each corner.

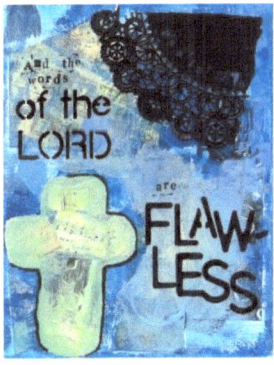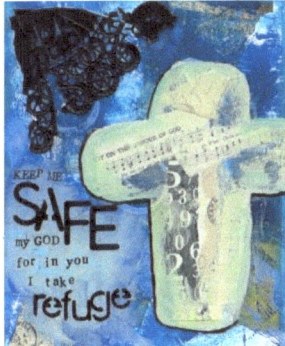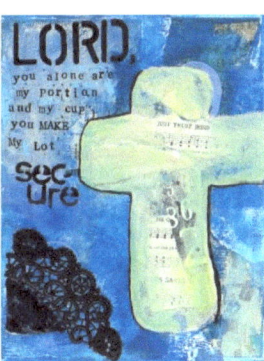

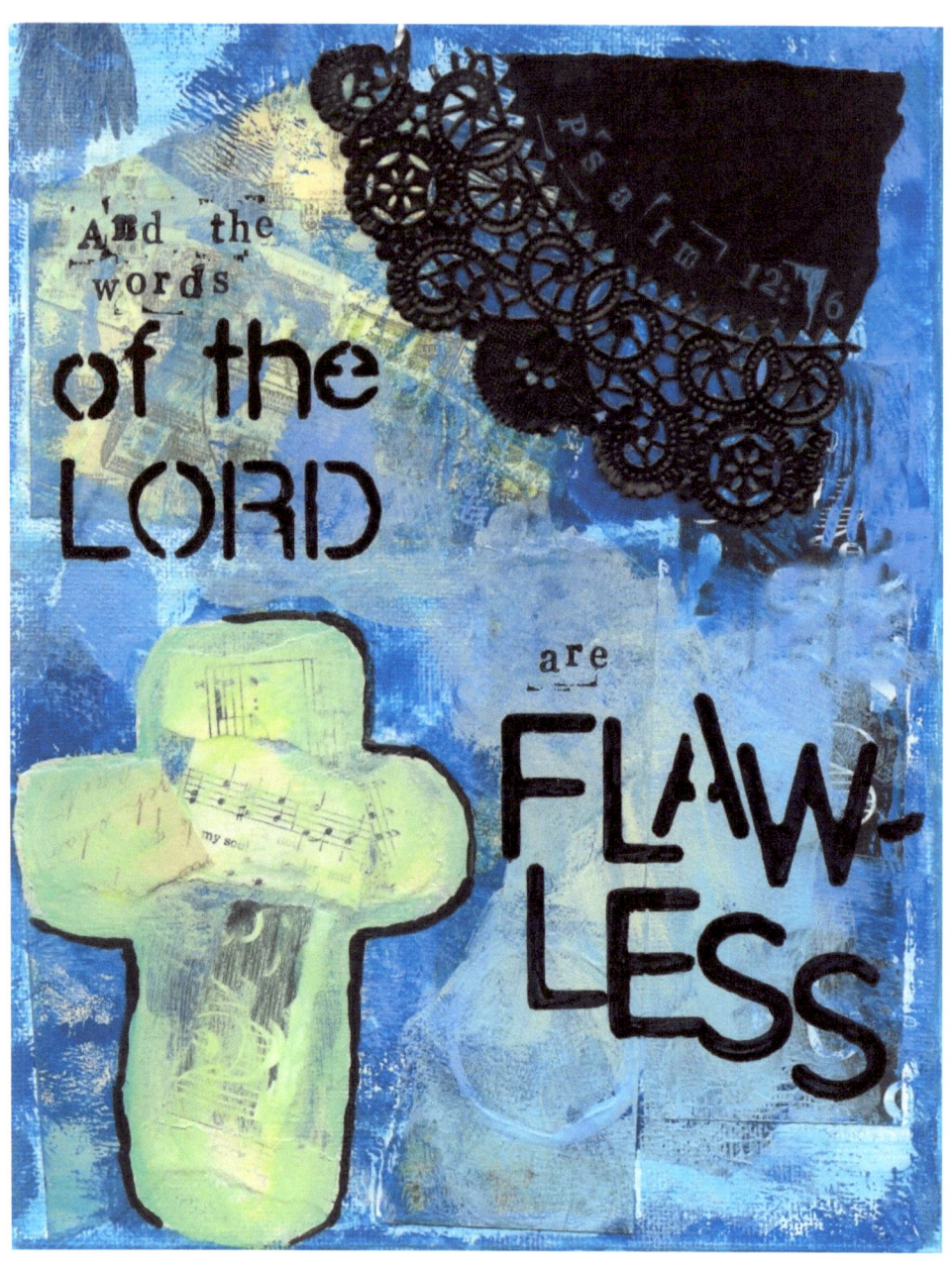

Cherie Burbach

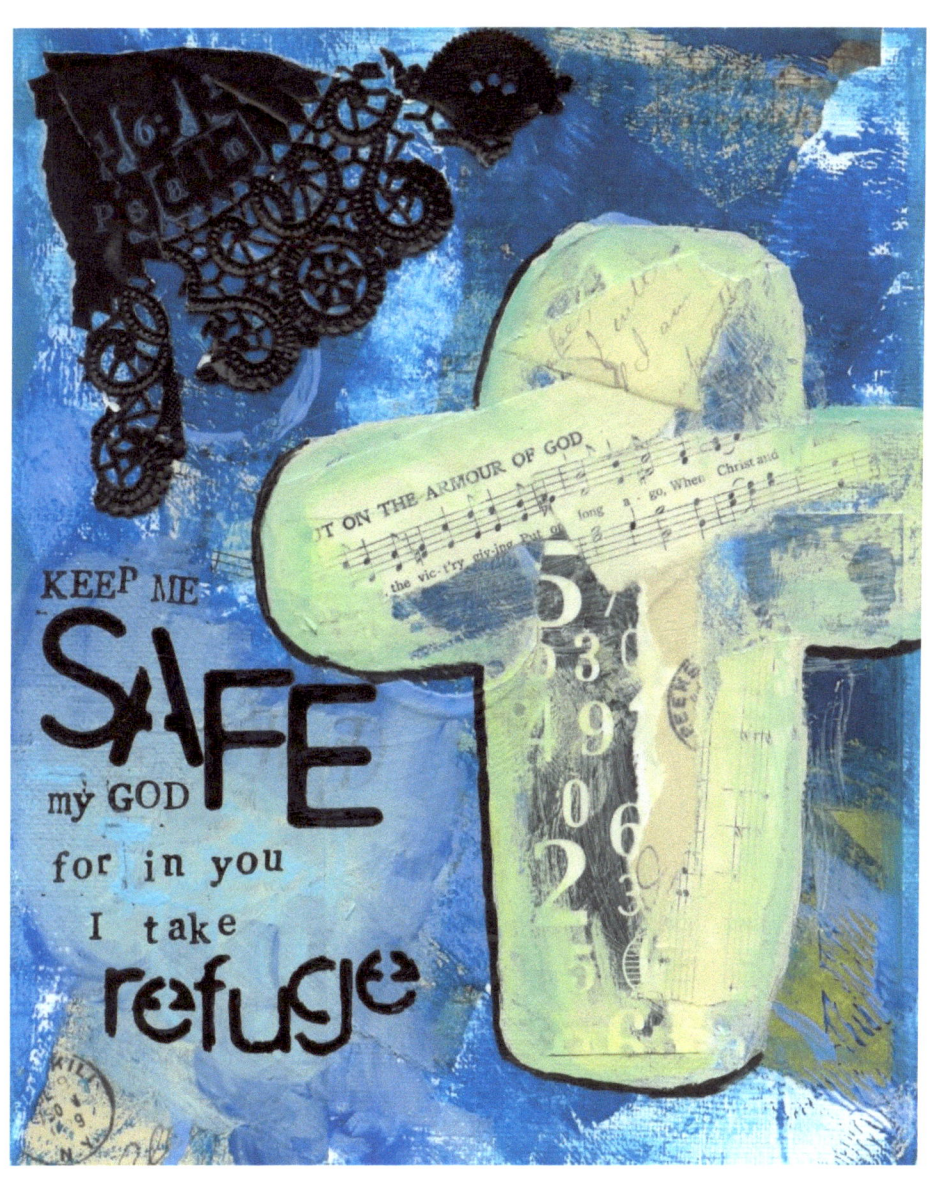

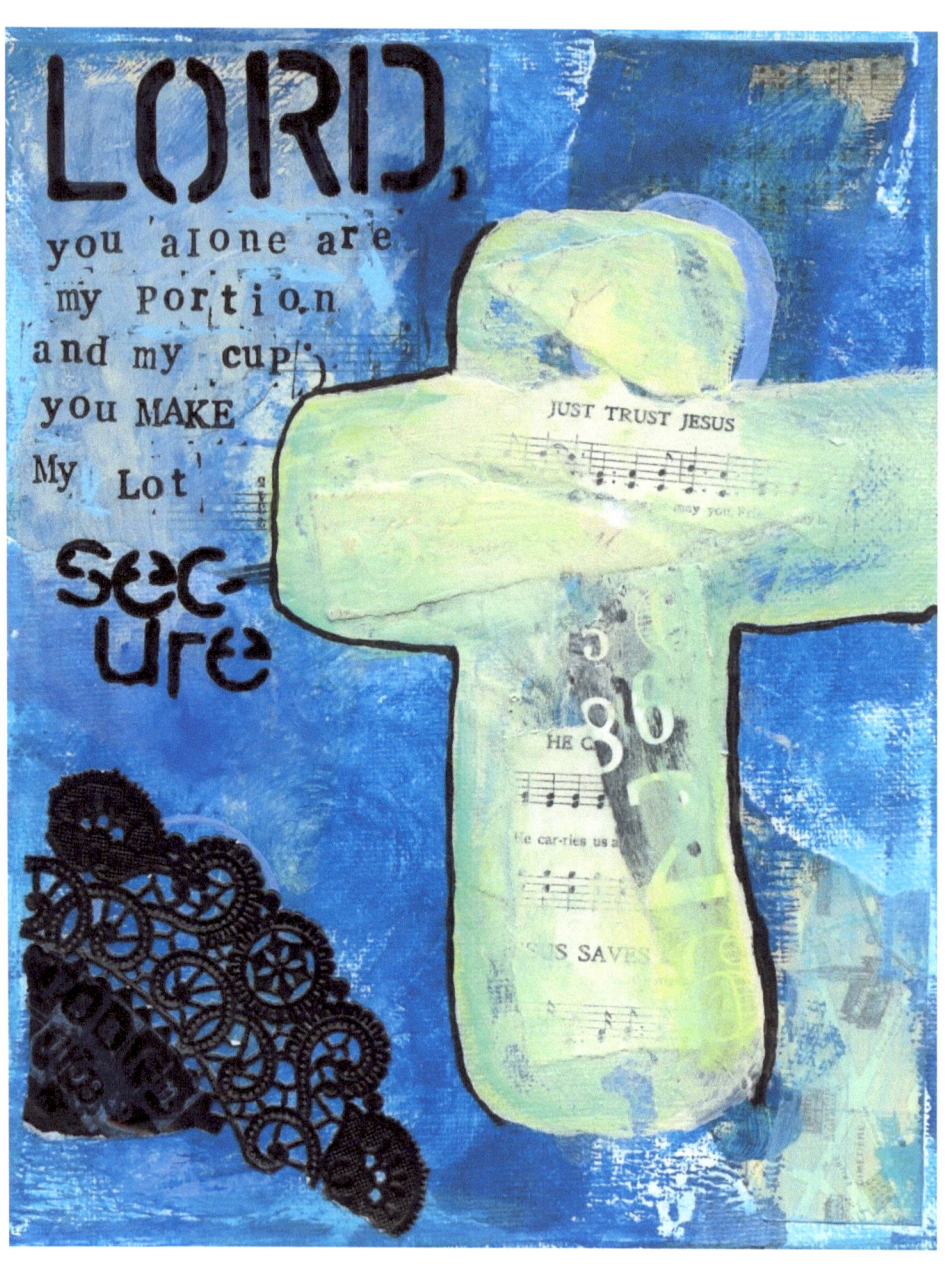

Cherie Burbach

Turning Your Ear to Wisdom

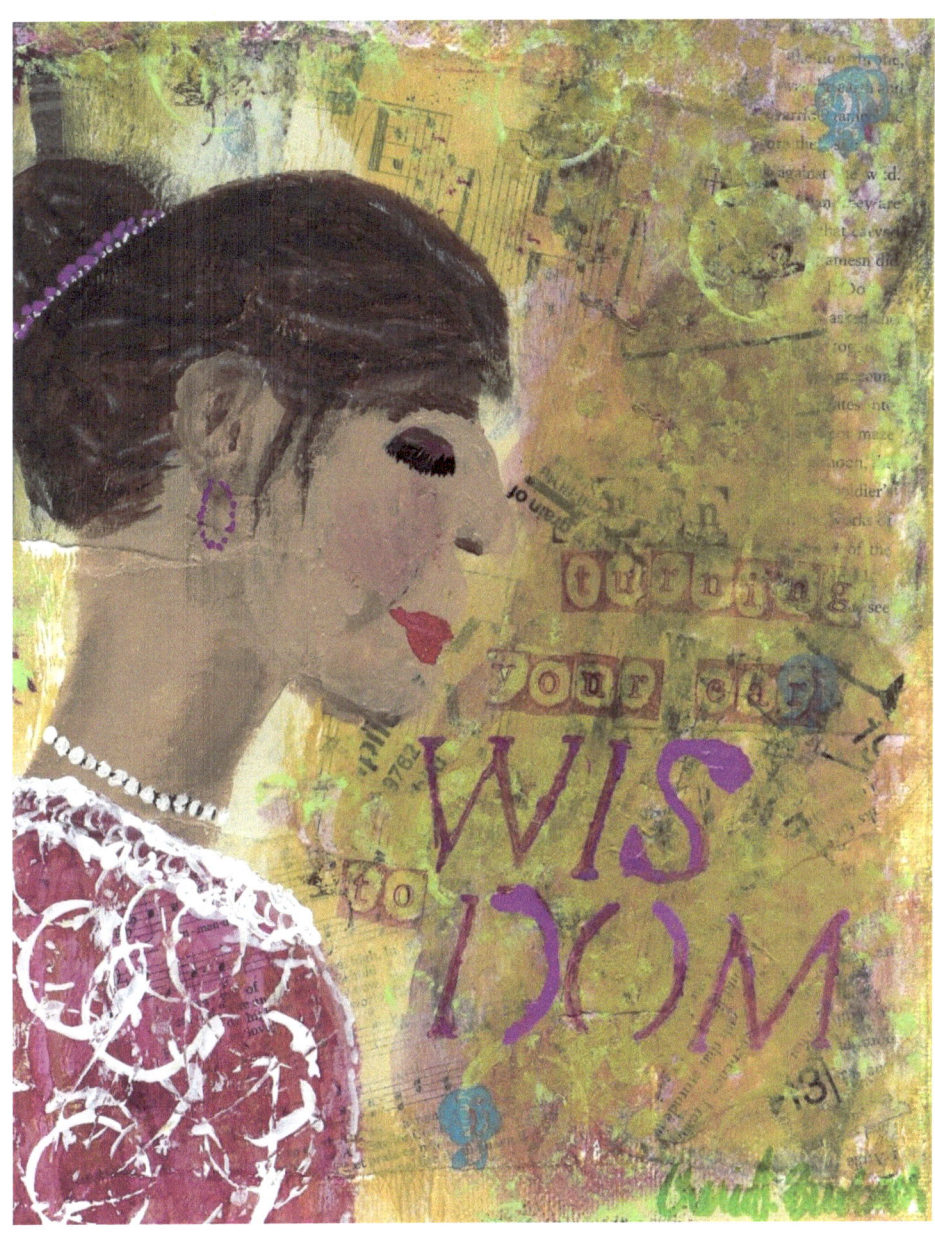

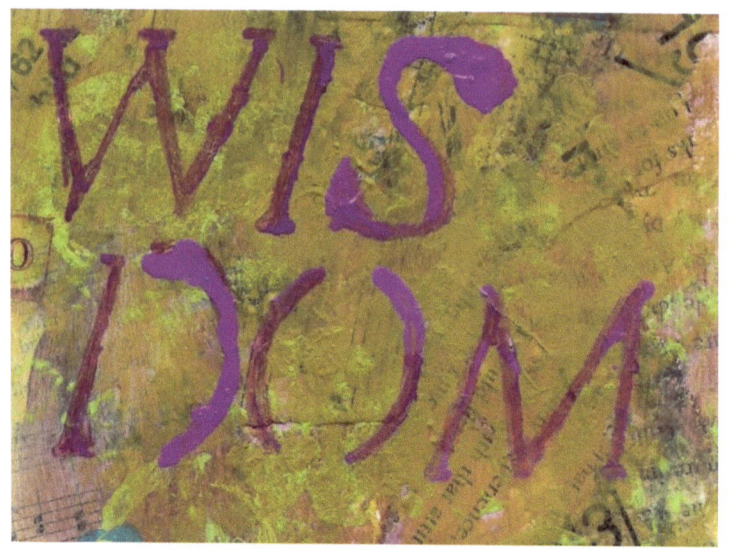

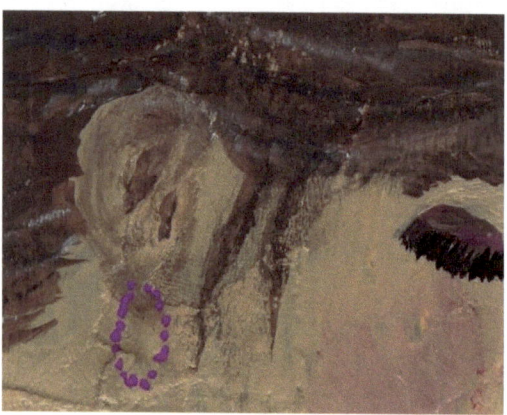

Listening to God… trying to figure out what He is telling you for your life. That can be difficult, especially in this world of loud voices and influences, people who freely offer opinions and pop culture and media that is in our faces all the time. There are times when I need to make a decision and pray for wisdom. Sometimes the ability to hear God's voice over everything else is one of the most challenging things, and "turning my ear to wisdom" is exactly what I need most.

Cherie Burbach

For I Know the Plans I Have for You

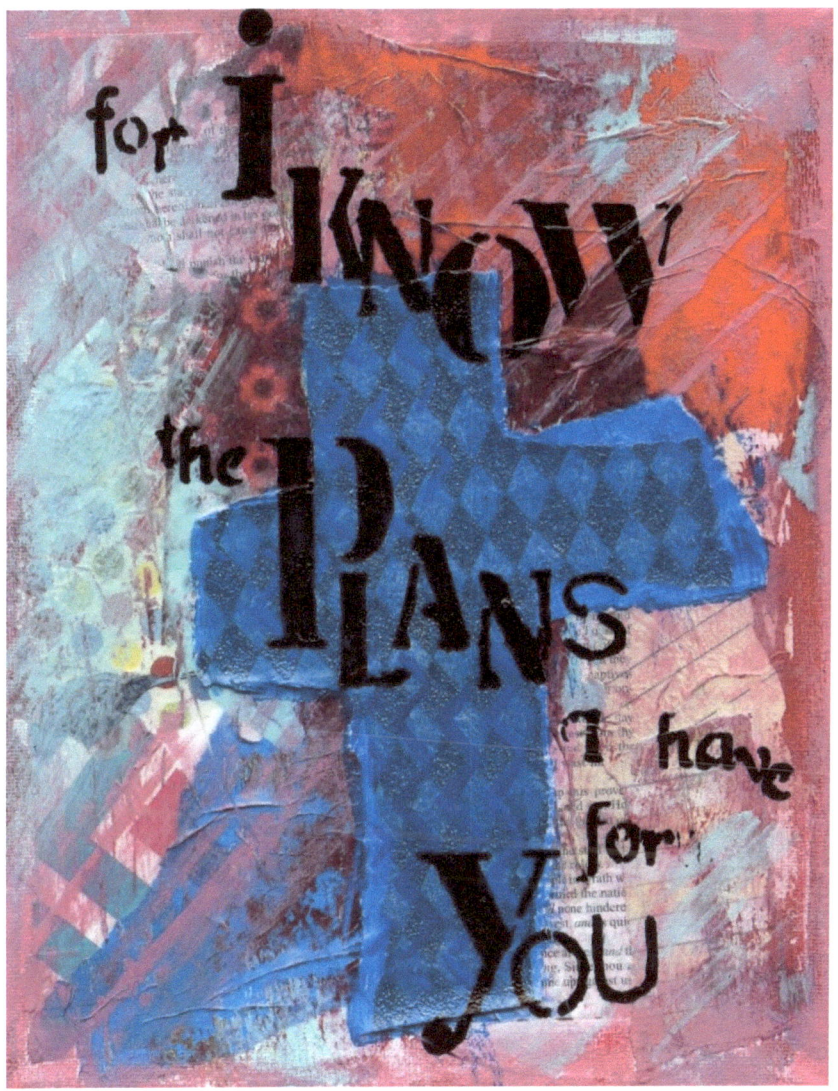

To know that God has a plan for our lives and our eternal future is the one thing we can go back to again and again when things are difficult.

There is a big picture we don't always see, we *can't* always see, but we can take comfort in the fact that God is in our charge of it.

Delight Yourself In the Lord

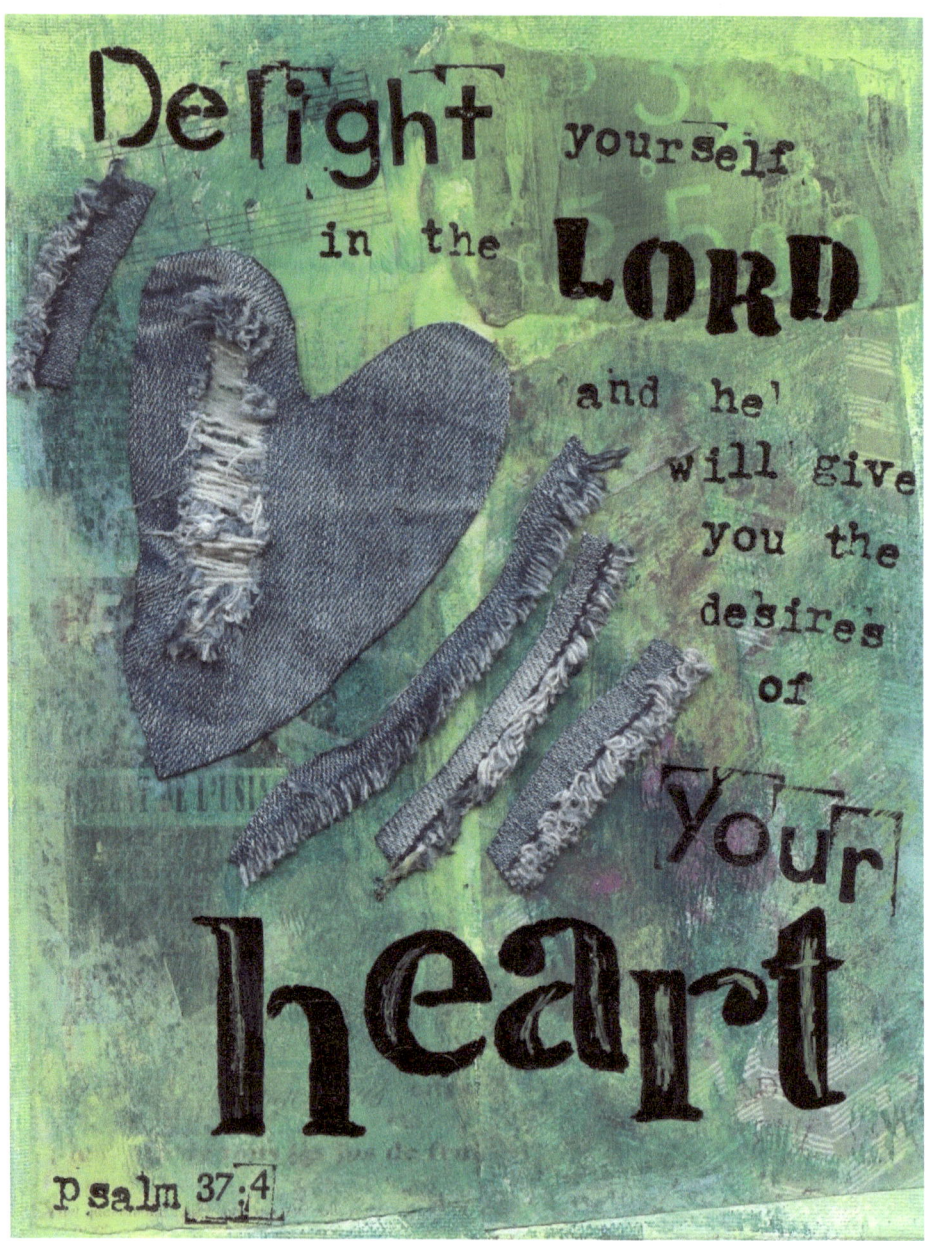

I've used this verse on quite a few paintings. It reminds me to pray for God's will for my life, which may look different than my own personal goals and dreams.

Cherie Burbach

I Will Lift Up My Eyes

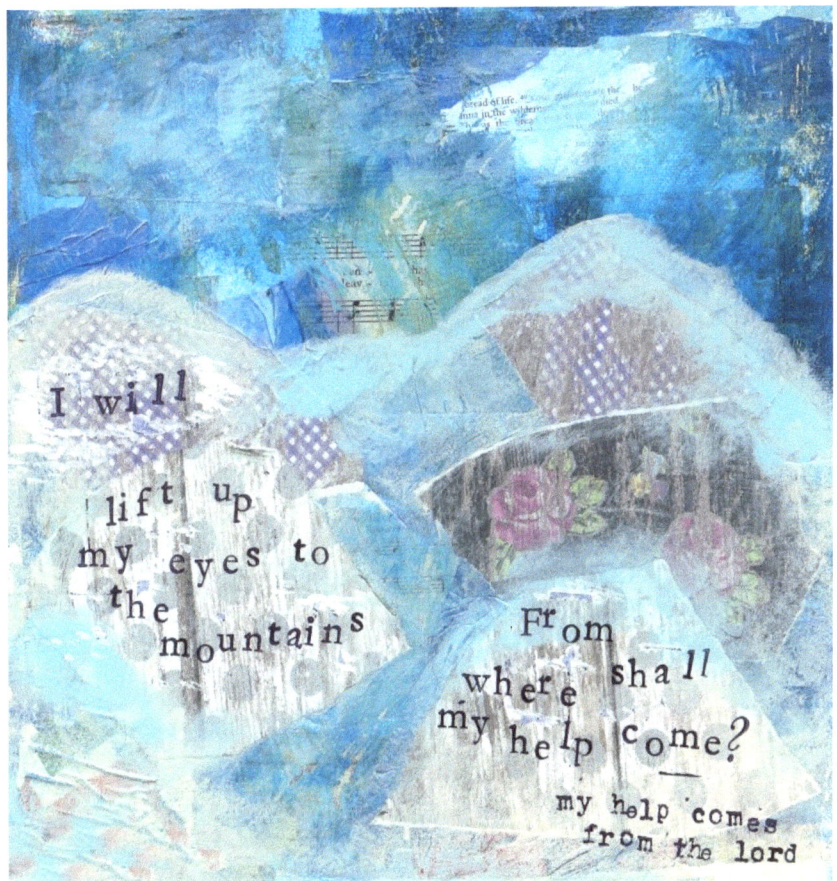

We look up when we look for God, even though He is everywhere. When I am feeling low and unimportant, I like to think of the mountains to remind myself that God created them *and* me. He created every wonder of this world and I am part of that. You can't help but to feel loved when you remember that.

For God So Loved the World

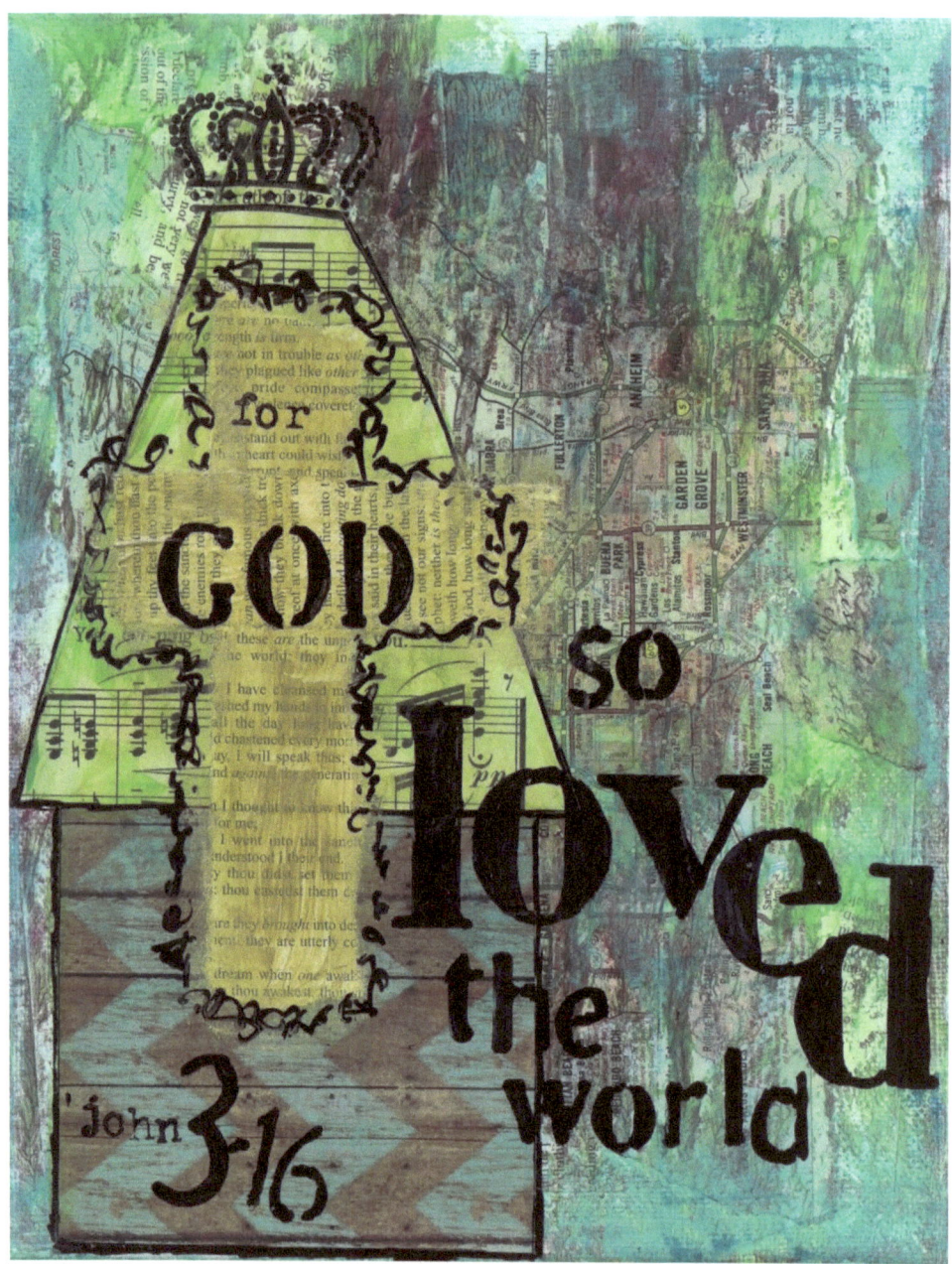

One of the most popular verses requested by people, and for good reason!

Cherie Burbach

Wedding Series: And They Shall Become One Flesh

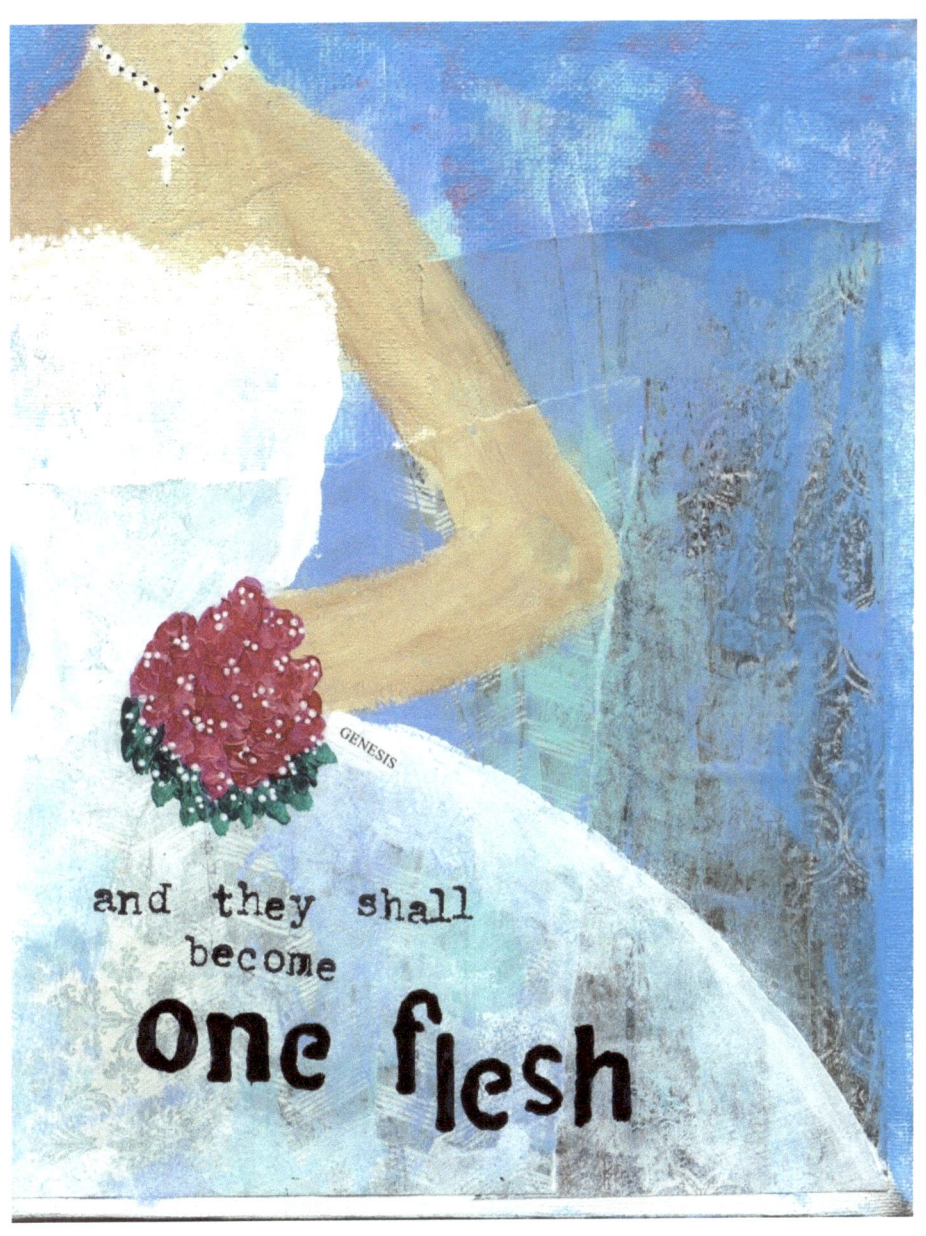

Wedding Series: All Things, Beloved, Steadfast Love

I love the idea of giving original art to a couple first starting out in marriage. I created this series that centers on brides and hopefulness and love. I wanted to remember the time I walked down the aisle and felt the love of my family and friends as I made my way down the alter to meet the man who would change my life, my husband and best friend.

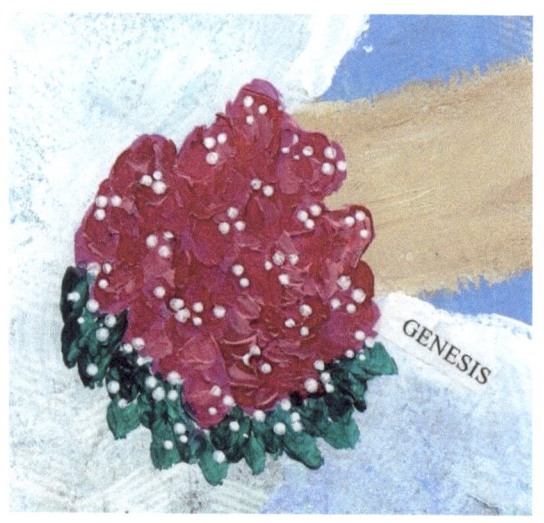

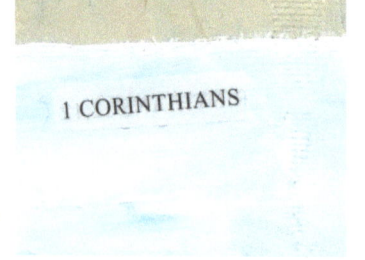

Cherie Burbach

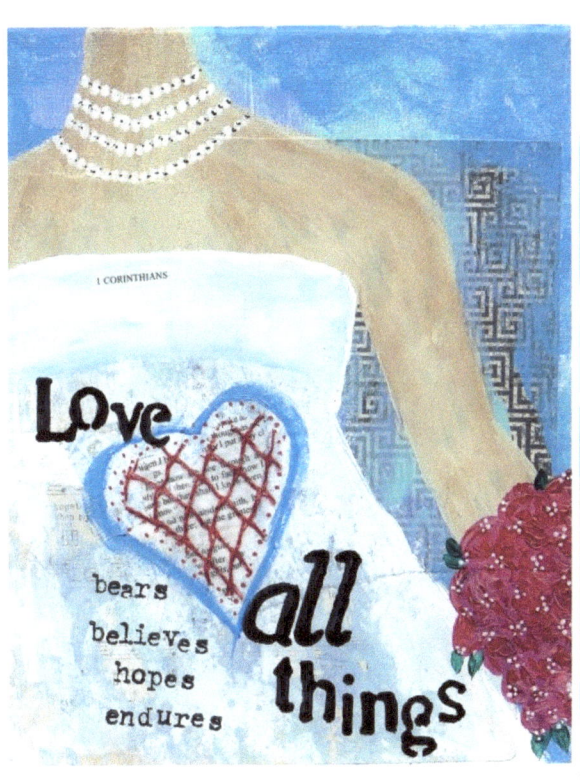

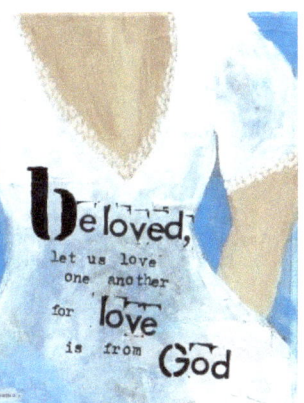

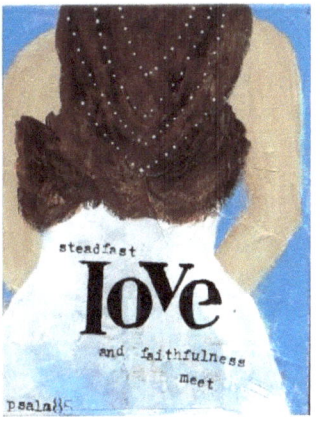

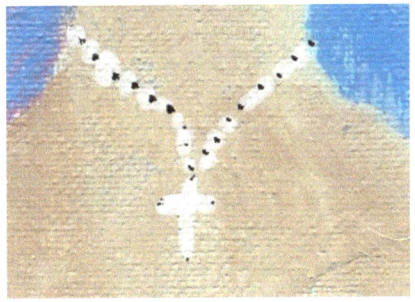

Bless the Lord O My Soul

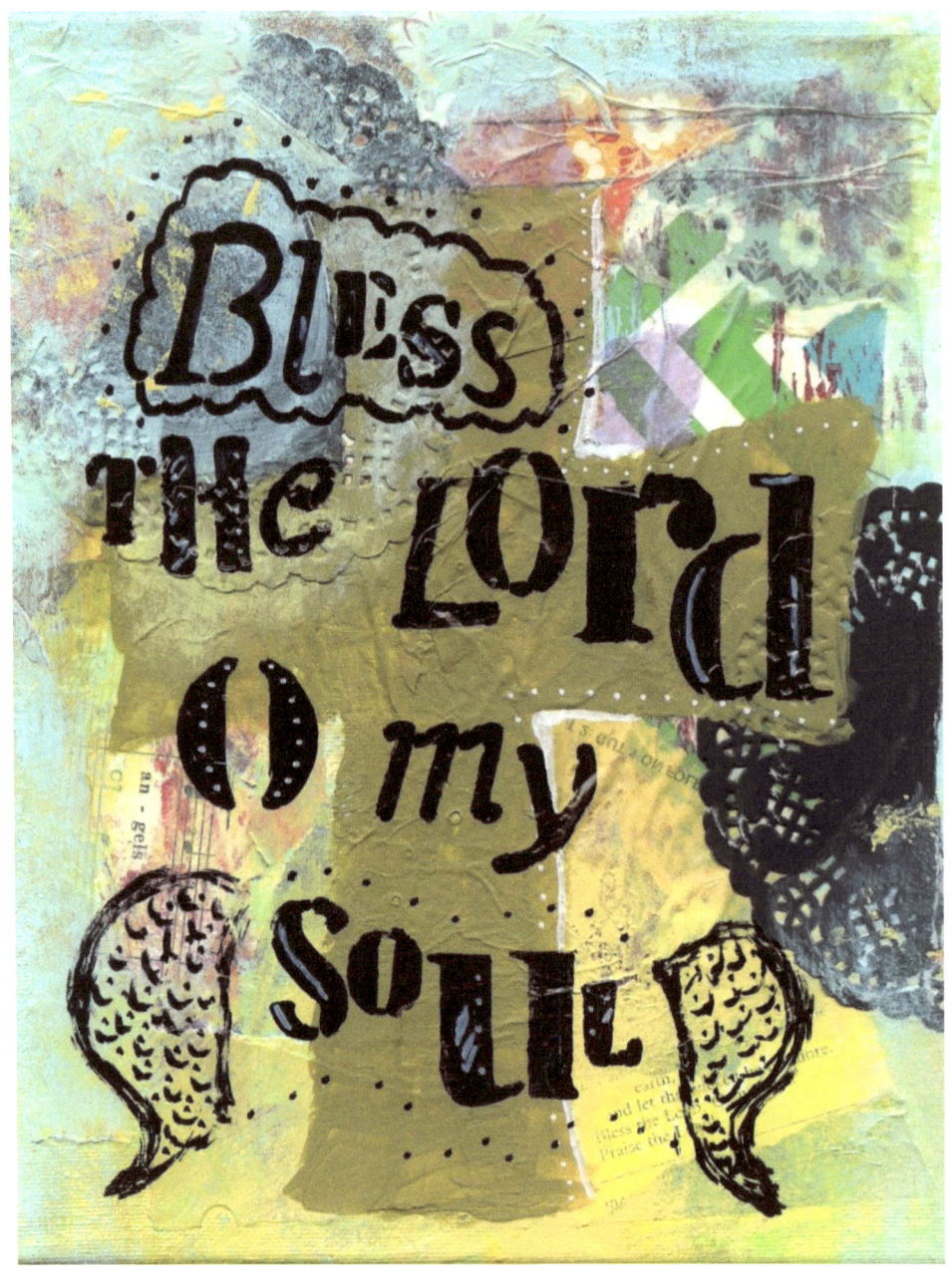

Cherie Burbach

The Psalms have remained my favorite part of the Bible. I love the poetry and emotion in them. I like that they show us a different side, the soulful side, to King David. When I was young I first gravitated toward these verses, and they have remained a place for me to find rest when I am weary, and find strength when I am feeling low.

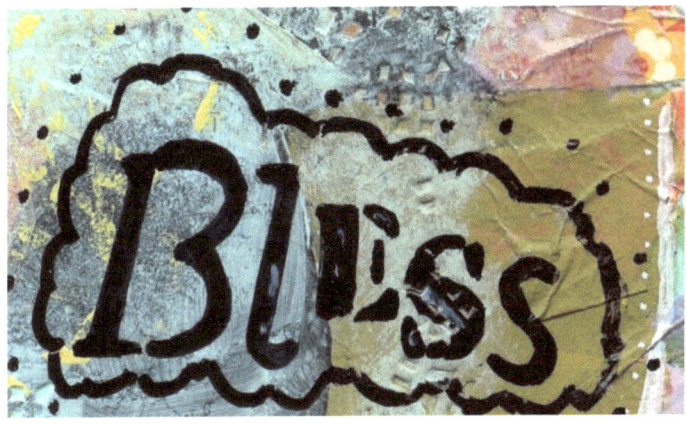

The Psalms also encourage celebration! In Psalms 103 it says, "Bless the Lord, O my soul: and all that is within me, bless his holy name." (King James Version)

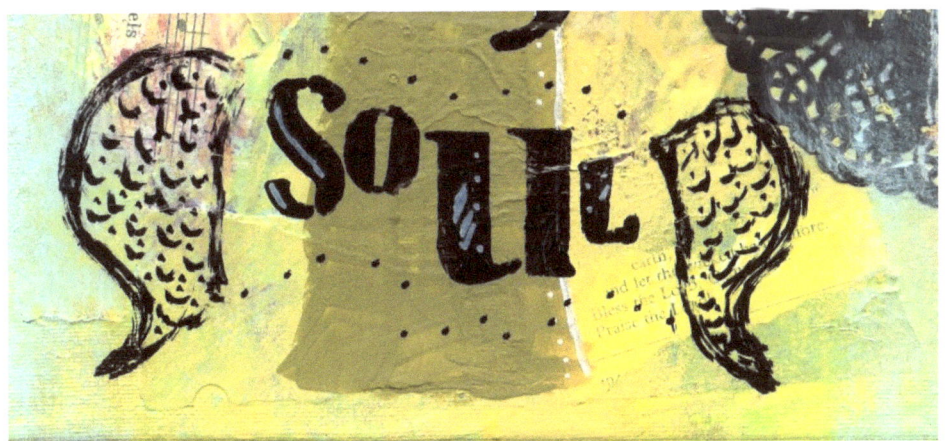

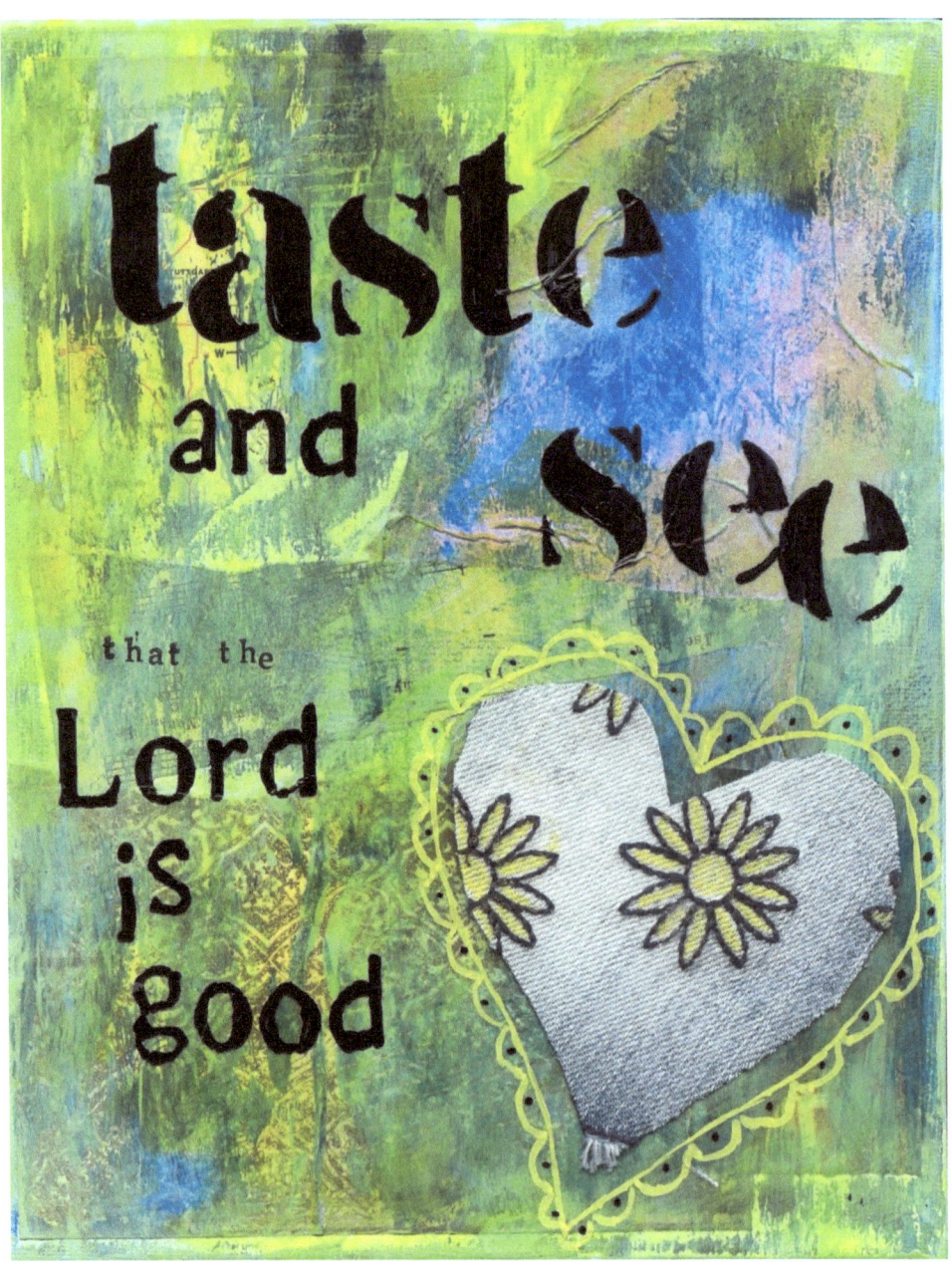

Cherie Burbach

Very often our most memorable experiences happen with a combination of senses. We enter a restaurant and the lighting adds to our experience enjoying the food. We go to a concert and the music gives off a vibe that moves us emotionally, not just with our ears but with our entire heart. The Lord provides us with so many things to experience His love and goodness, from the hug of someone who has just prayed for you to the songs we sing to rejoice His ability to transform our lives.

And He Said to Them

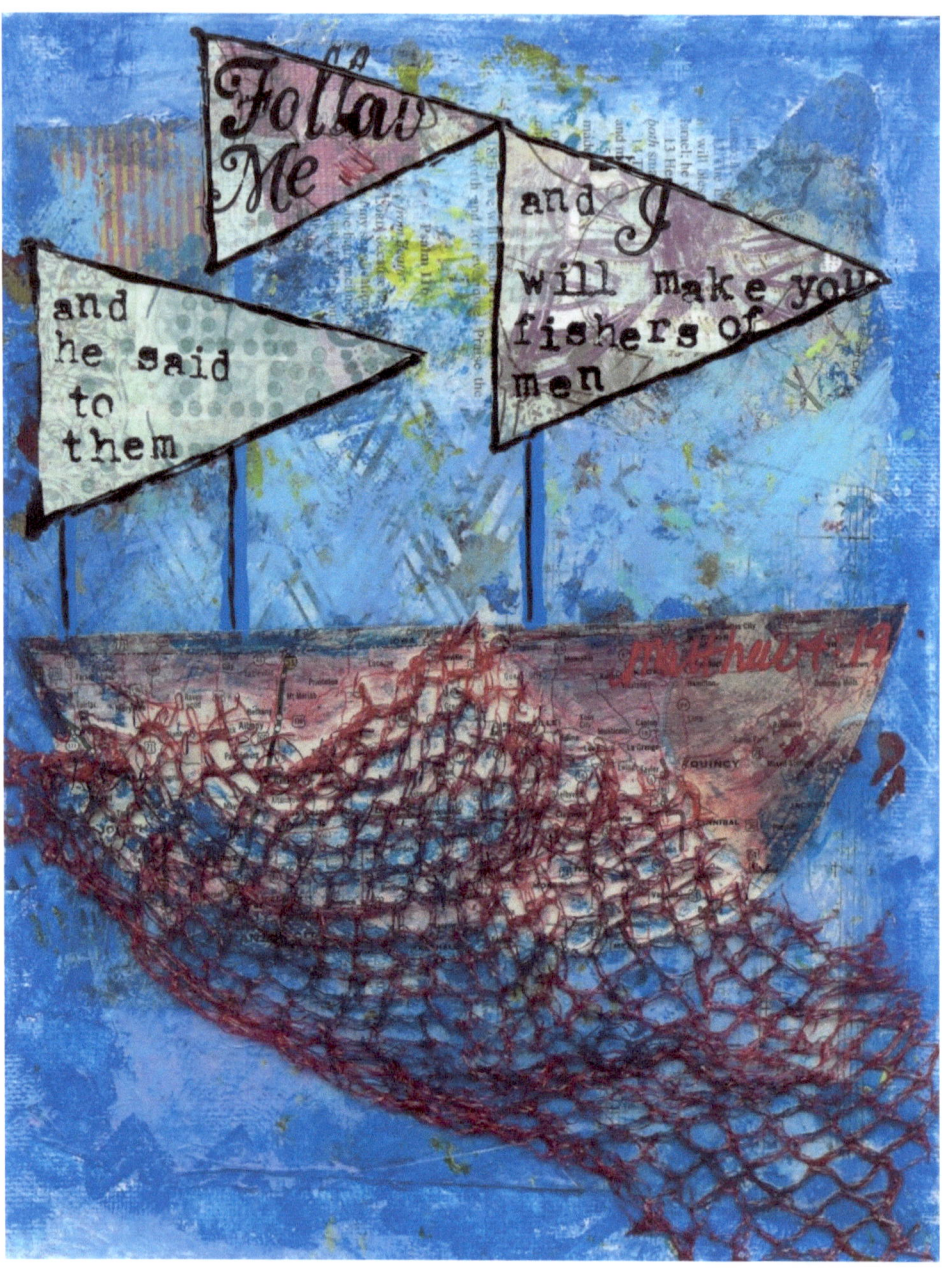

Cherie Burbach

That I May Dwell

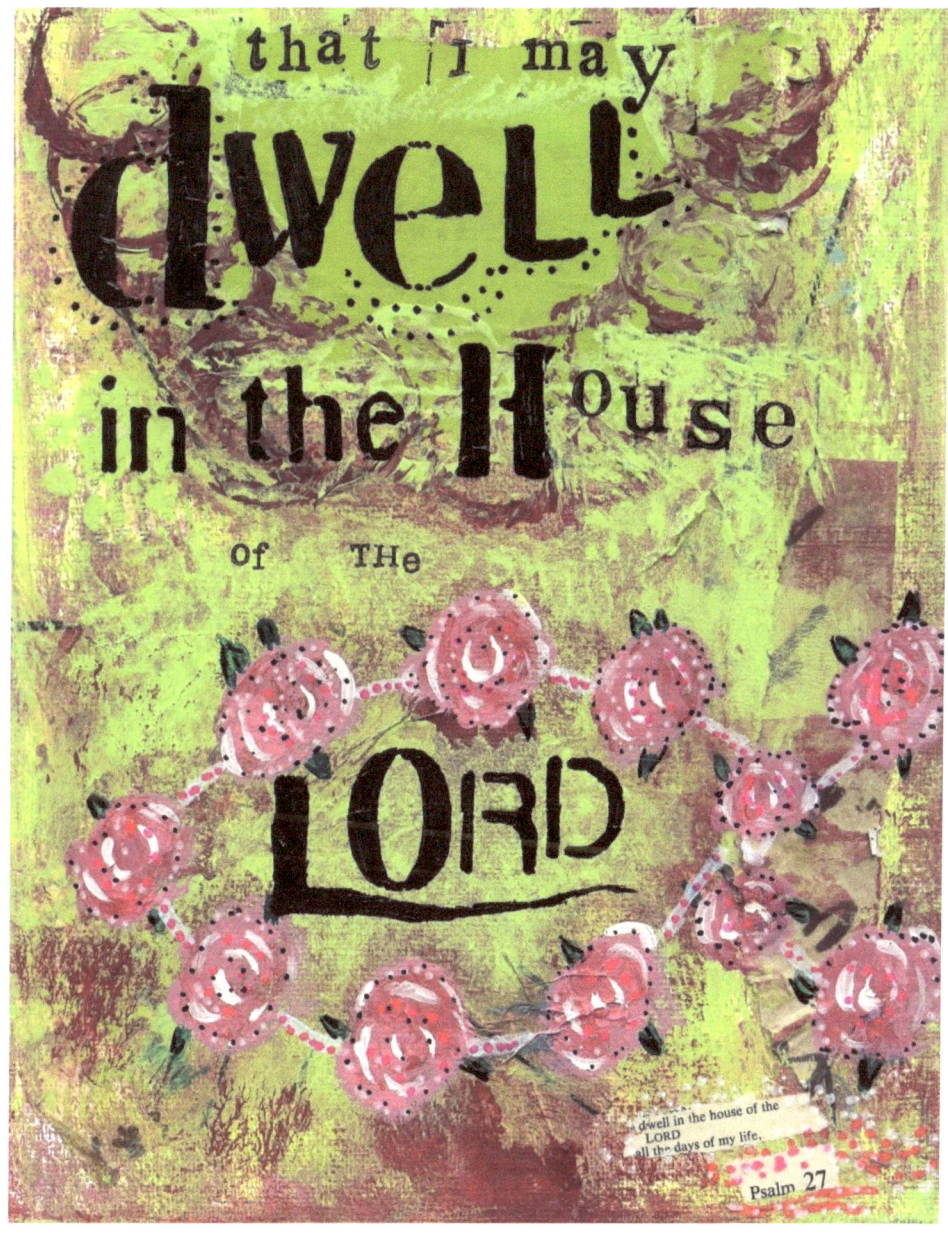

that I may dwell in the House of the LORD

dwell in the house of the
LORD
all the days of my life.

Psalm 27

This verse gives me comfort. When I'm feeling low or wondering where life is taking me, I can rest in this verse, knowing that whatever happens now, in the end I will dwell in the house of the Lord, forever.

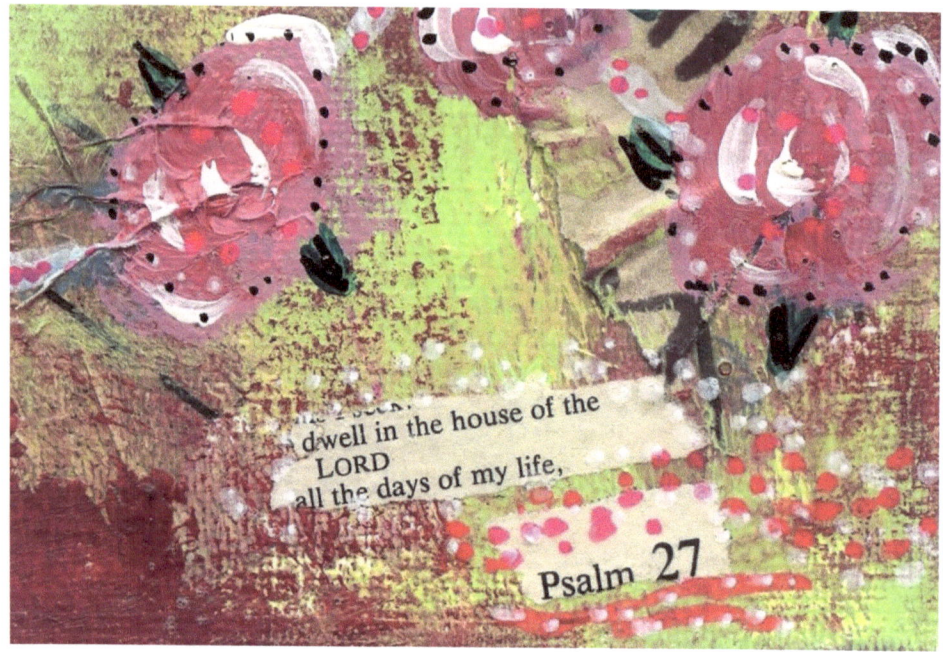

Cherie Burbach

King of Glory

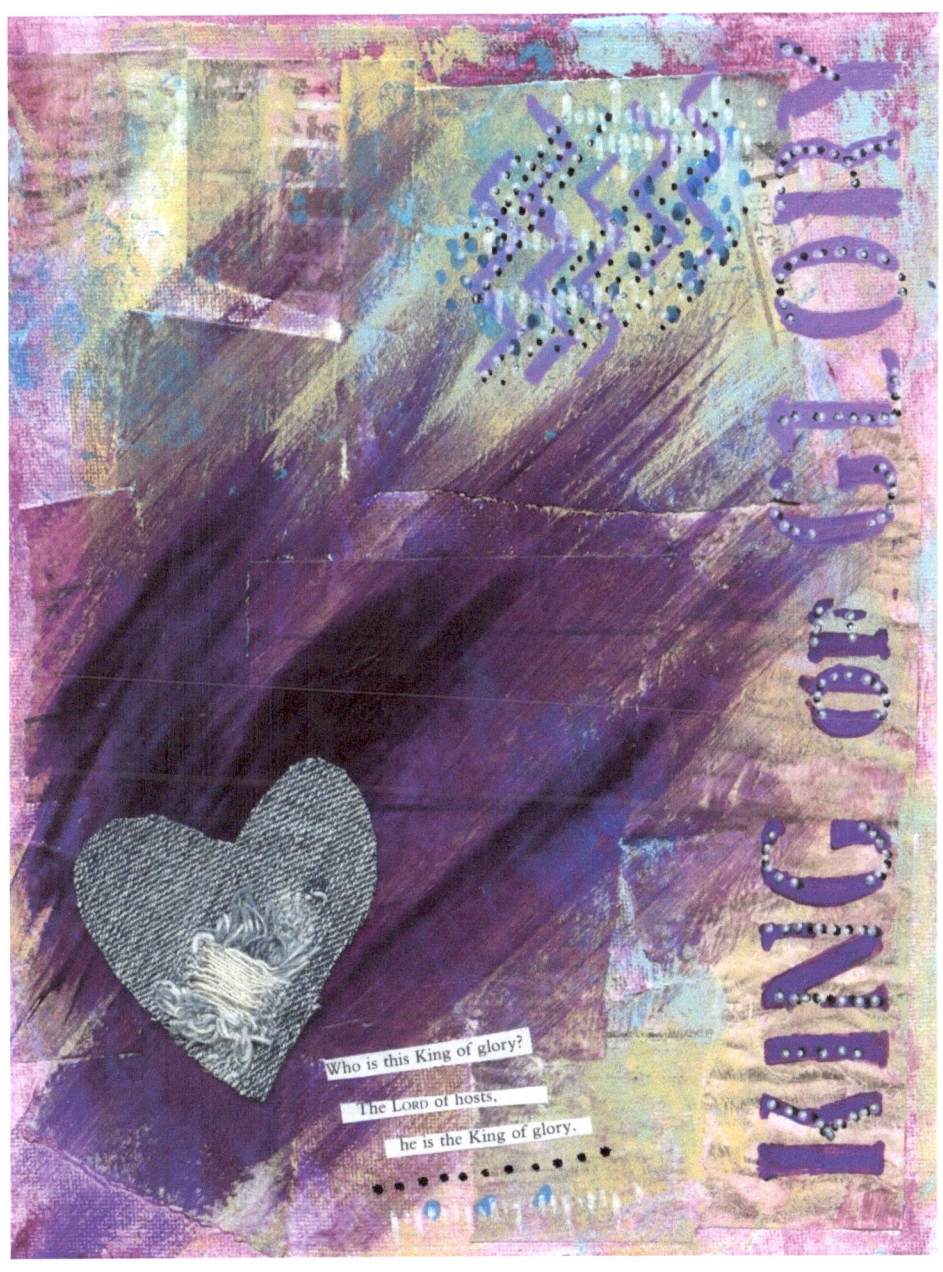

Who is this King of glory?
The LORD of hosts,
he is the King of glory.

Who is this King of glory? Strong and mighty!

I can't imagine what it would feel like to know that you were in the presence of Jesus Christ, that he was here, in the flesh, come to earth at the same time you were there. I can't imagine the wonder and bewilderment and joy the disciples must have felt as they witnessed miracles and learned what it really means to show love.

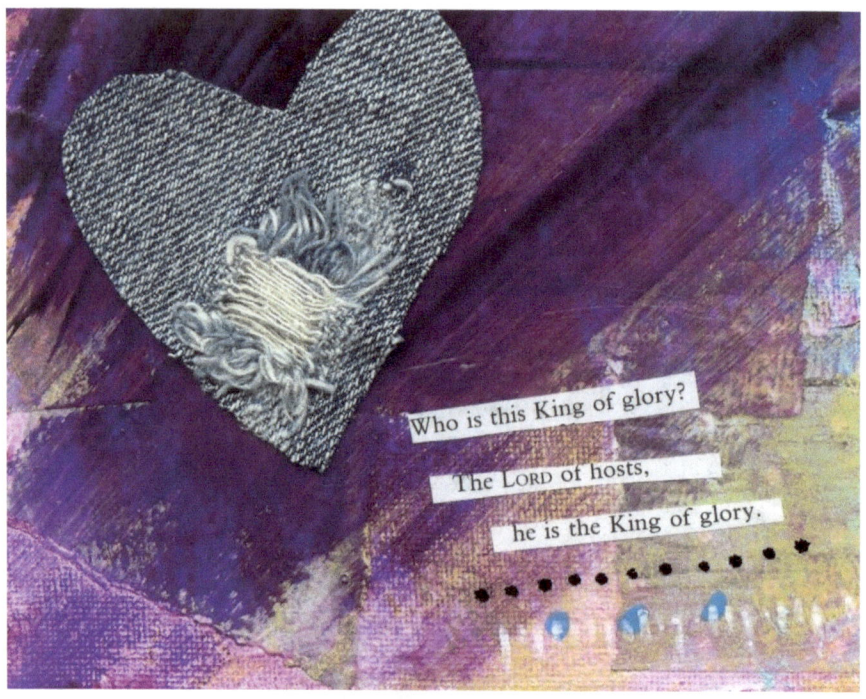

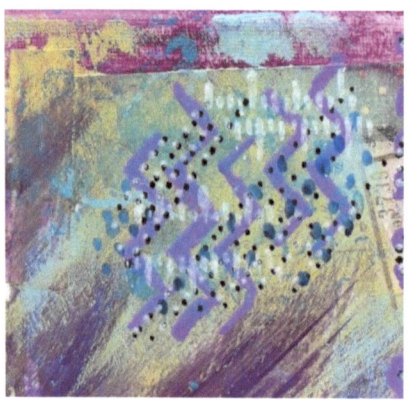

Cherie Burbach

In the Beginning God Created

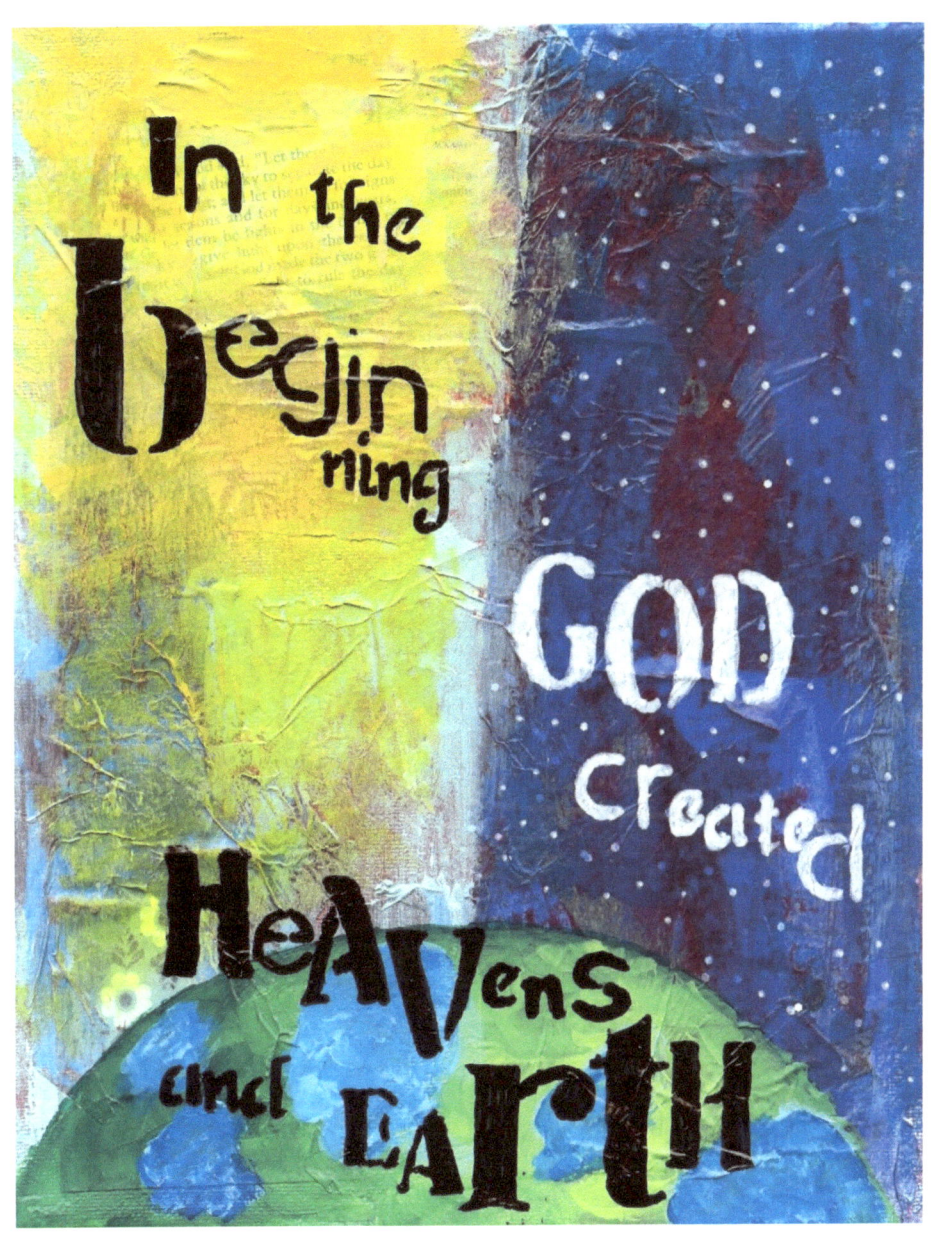

I've always been a fan of the creation story, but recently I saw a video that really made it stand out to me in a completely new way.

In 1968, the Apollo 8 astronauts orbited the moon on Christmas Day, and as their flight was broadcast they read from the book of Genesis, starting with the creation story. Seeing this perspective that most of us won't get to see, of a dark universe and the earth in the distance, puts the creation story in 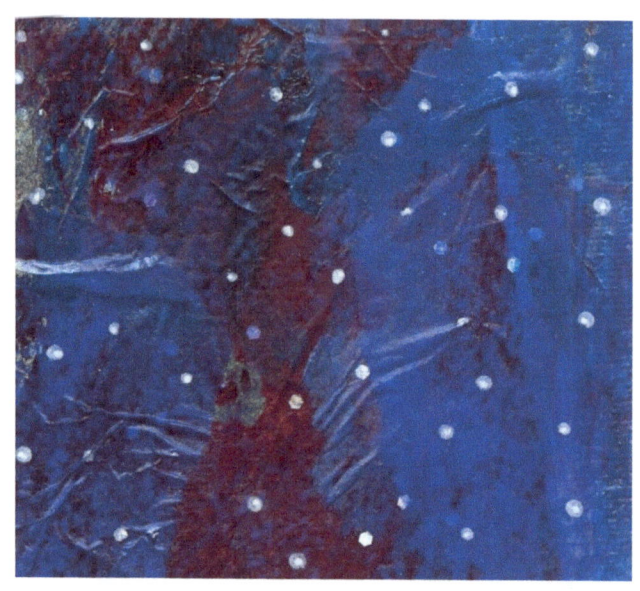 perspective for me. Imagine the darkness… until God created a world, for us… for *us*. What a miracle. (The Apollo 8 video is available if you search on YouTube. I highly recommend it!)

Cherie Burbach

Let Mutual Love Continue

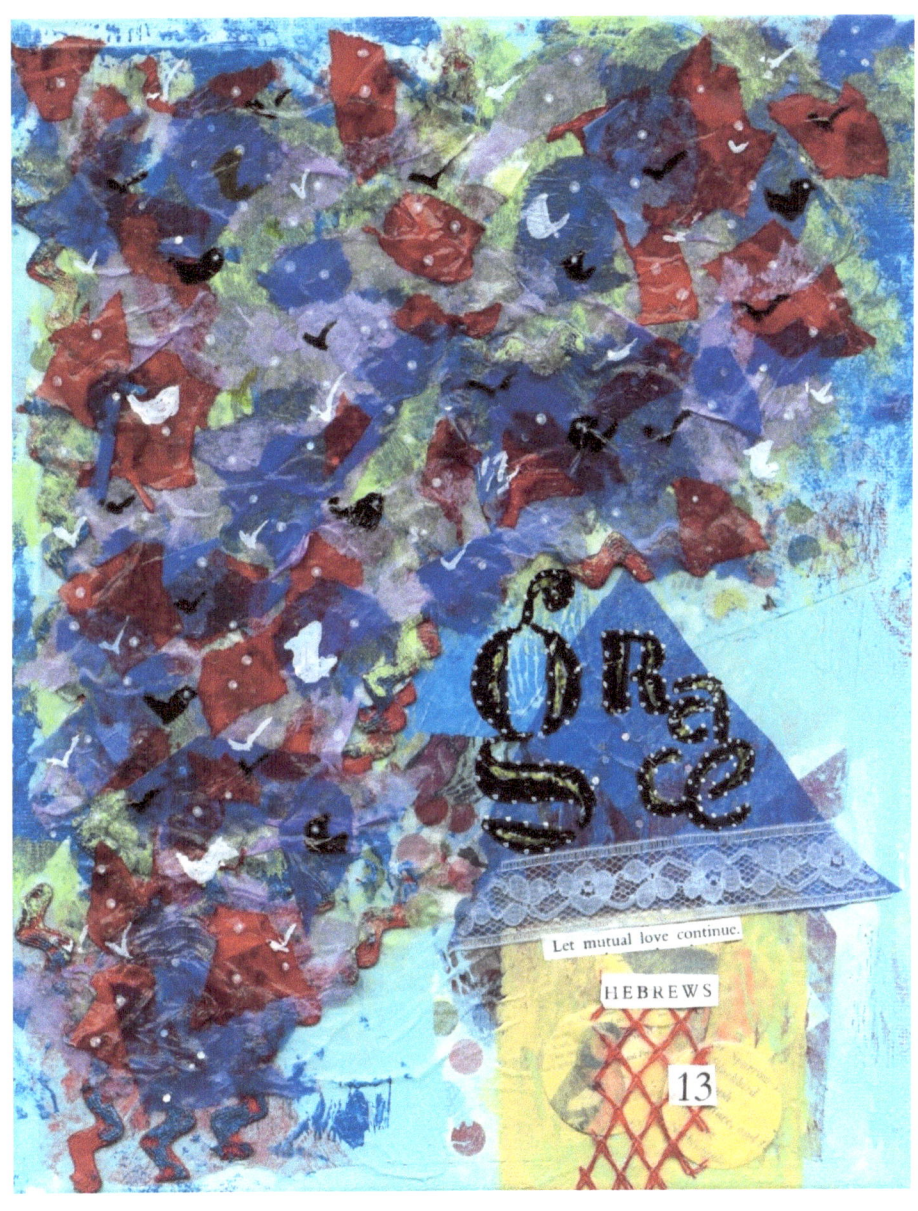

I like the thought of a house surrounded by grace, with the love of our brothers and sisters evident each time we step inside. A house that is a safe place, where we are loved and accepted. We have that with Jesus, but we are urged to provide this love to each other as well.

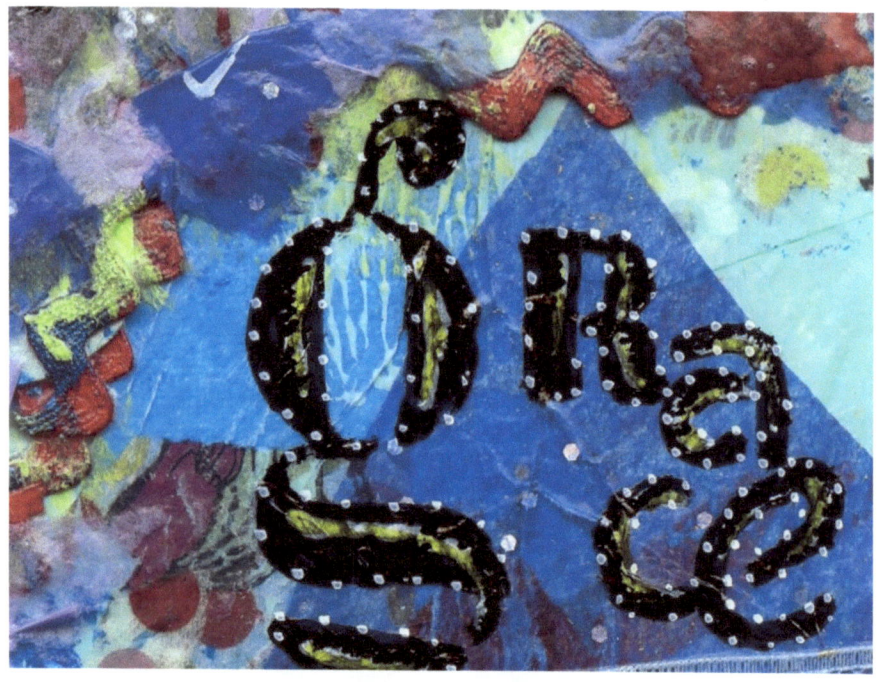

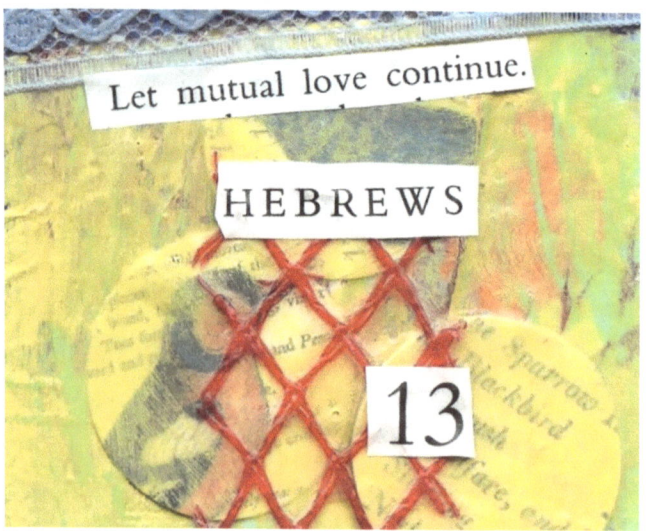

Cherie Burbach

Act Justly

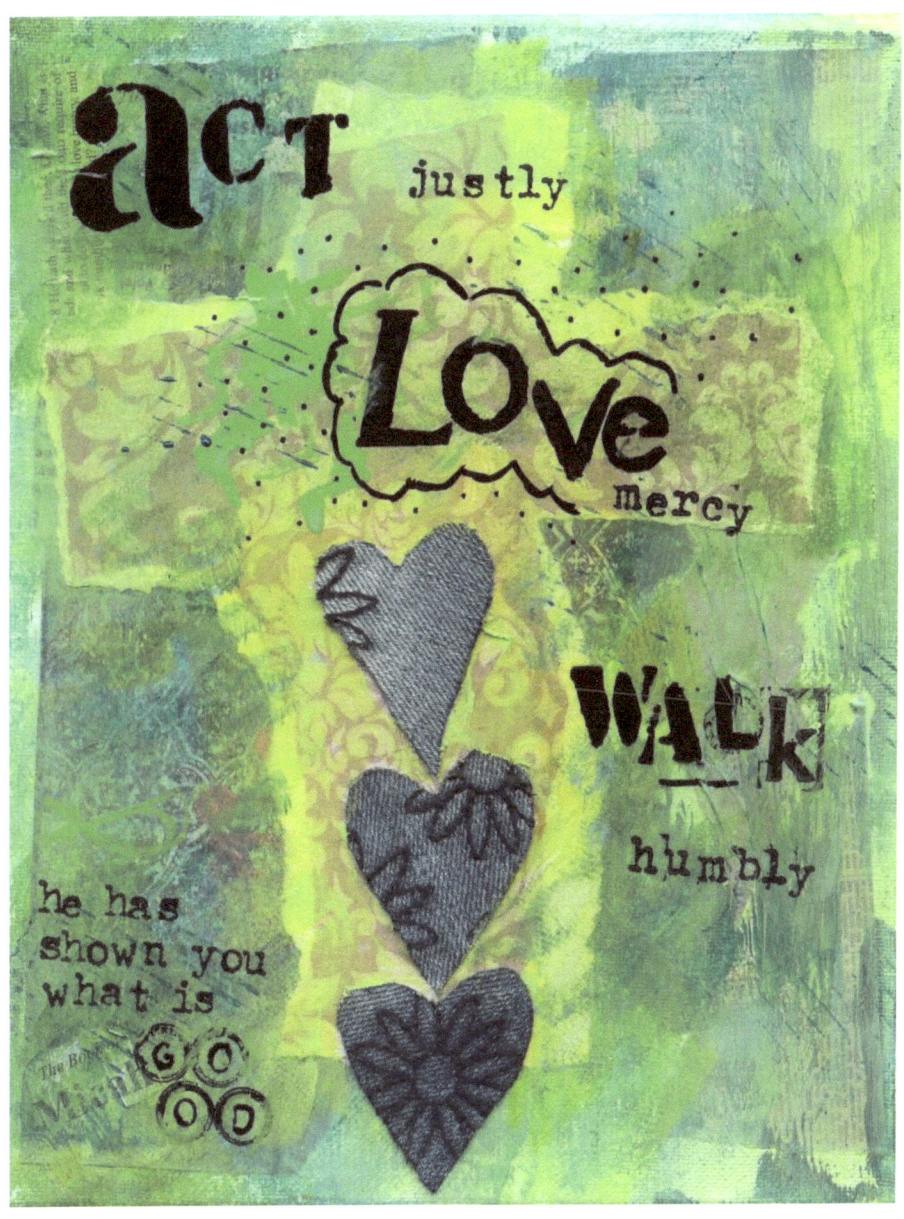

A Heart at Peace

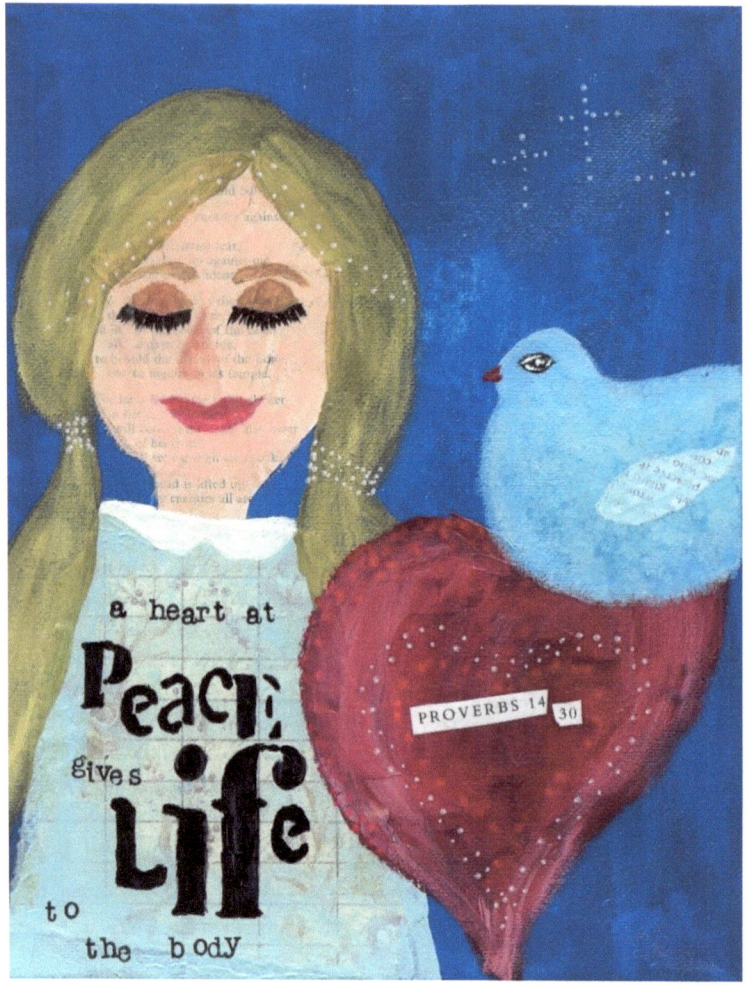

When you're not at peace with people and situations, it eats you up. There is a relief that comes from just forgiving and letting things go. It isn't always easy, but when someone hurts you the only way to find peace is through God. I ask Him to help me through it, and He makes things happen that I wouldn't have been able to do on my own. And even if you can't have peace with someone, God will help you find the kind of solace that "gives life" to your body and mind.

Cherie Burbach

Peace I Leave With You and My Peace I Give You

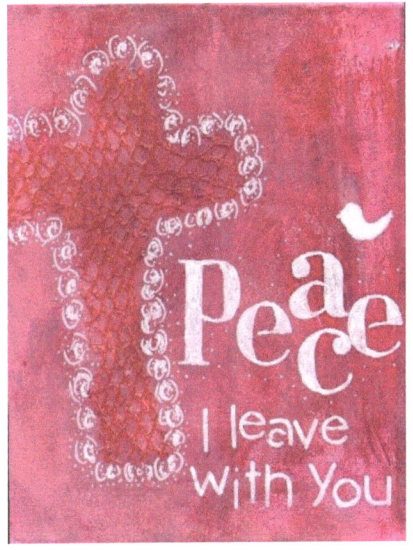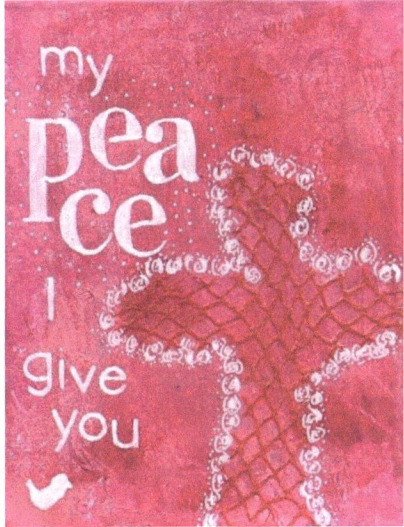

There is a lot of talk about peace in the Bible, especially as it relates to Jesus. The word peace is mentioned hundreds of times depending on which version you read, and for good reason. He is the shepherd that knows what we need to calm us and make us bold and unafraid. He tells us again and again, *lean on me, learn from me, seek me out…*

It seems fitting that this beautiful verse is included in John (14:27). John's poetic way of expressing his witness testimony shows us the beauty in Jesus' life and words. The NIV version of this verse says, "Peace I leave with you; my peace I give you. I do not give to you as the world gives. Do not let your hearts be troubled and do not be afraid." I like everything this version describes, right down to the part about fear. Jesus knows we will have troubles and keep negative thoughts in our hearts and minds but He tells us to simply come to Him, rest in Him.

Pray Without Ceasing

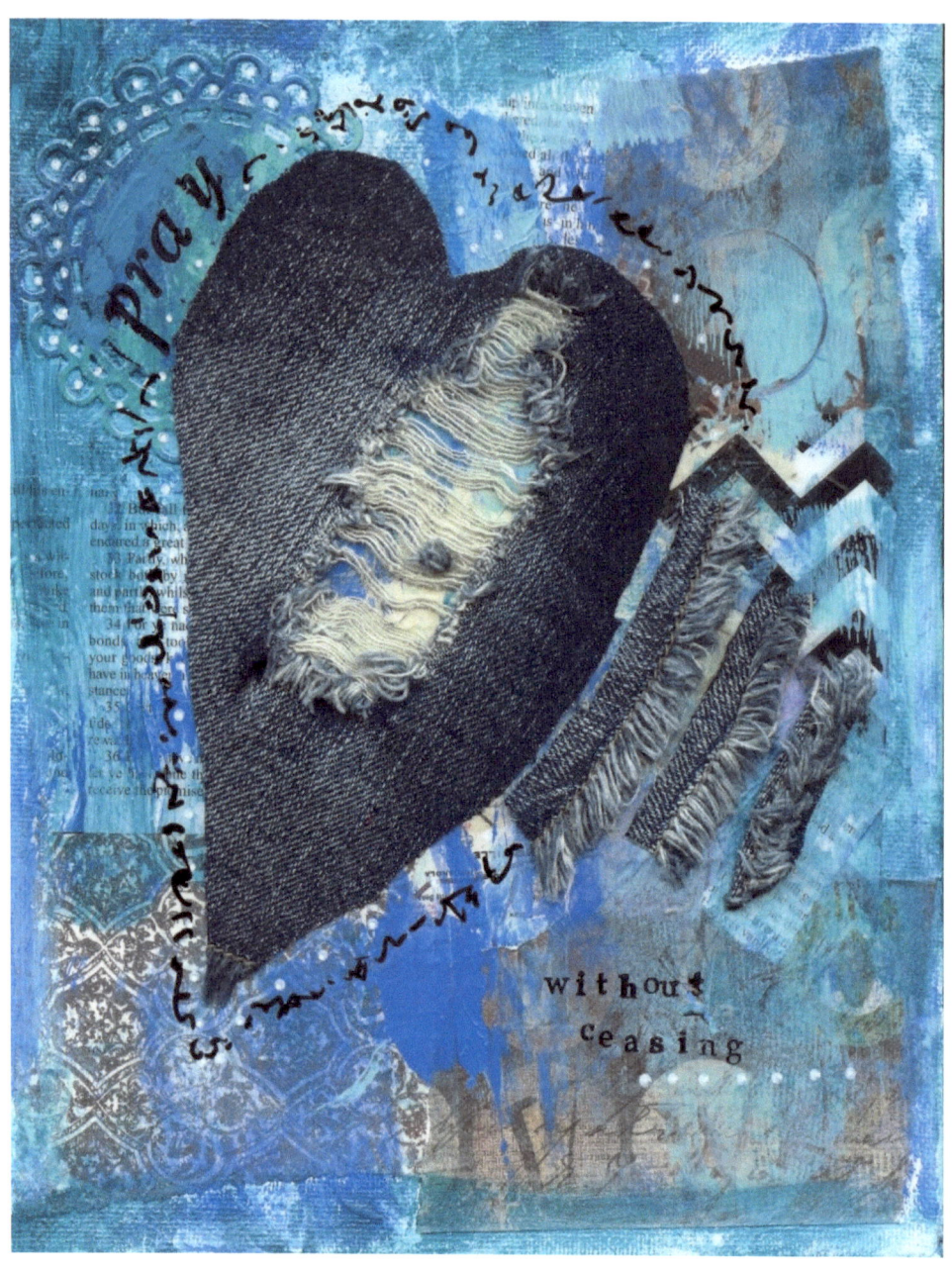

Cherie Burbach

My prayer life has changed a lot since I was a kid. I used to pray every night before I went to sleep. Now, I try and pray in the mornings to help center myself for the day ahead, and I also try and stop and say a prayer based on the things that come up during the day. Being able to reach out anytime and talk with God is one of life's biggest blessings. He is always there for us for whatever we need, whether it is to listen to our request or just to give us comfort when we cry out in hurt or frustration.

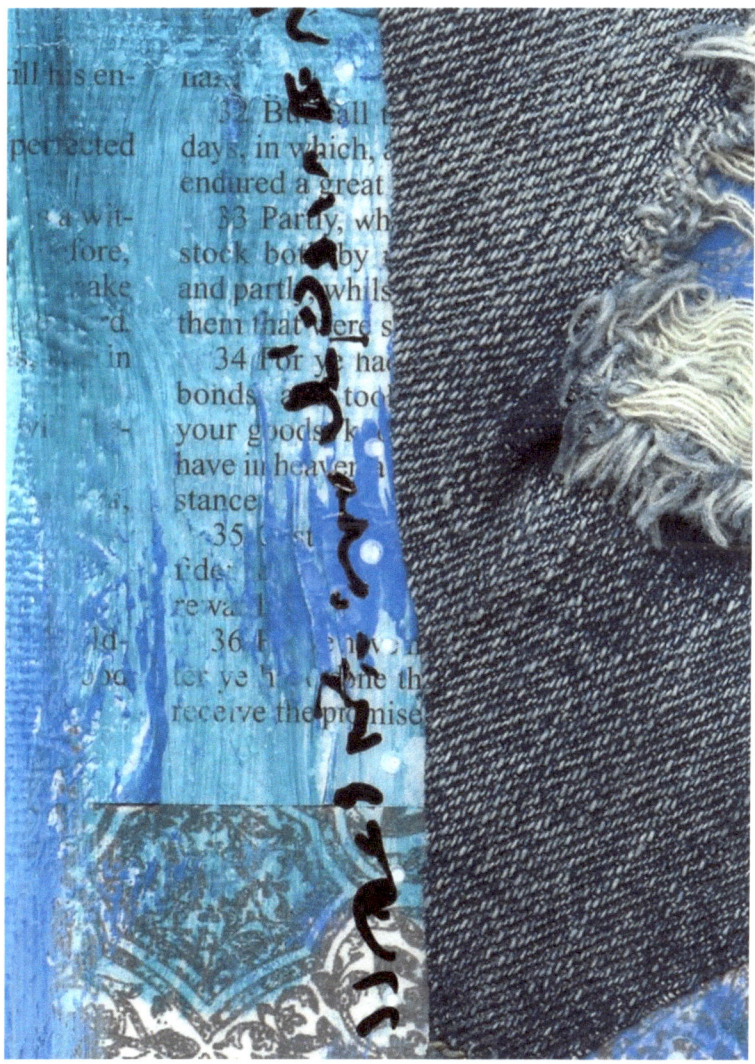

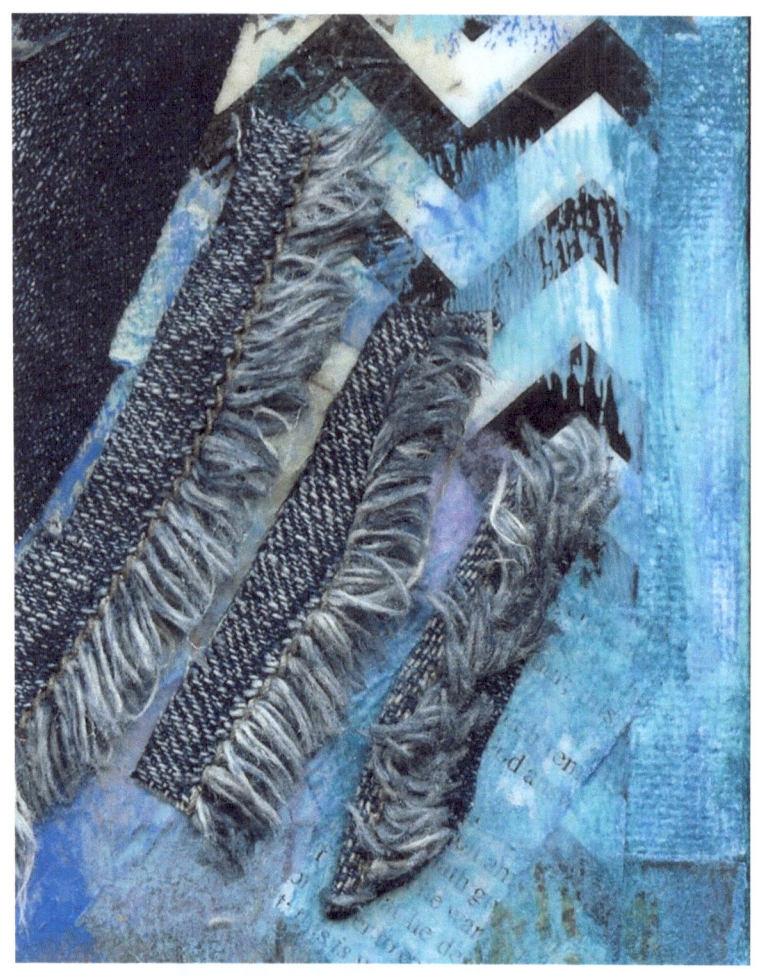

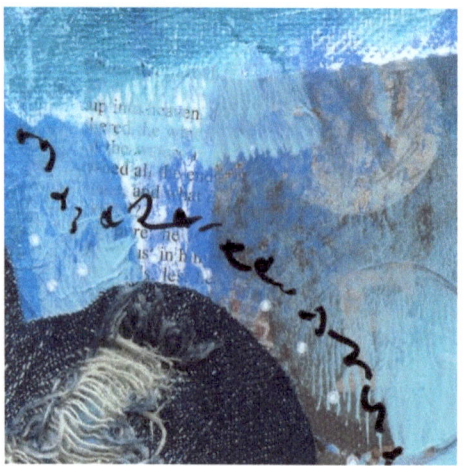

Cherie Burbach

The Heavenly Call of God

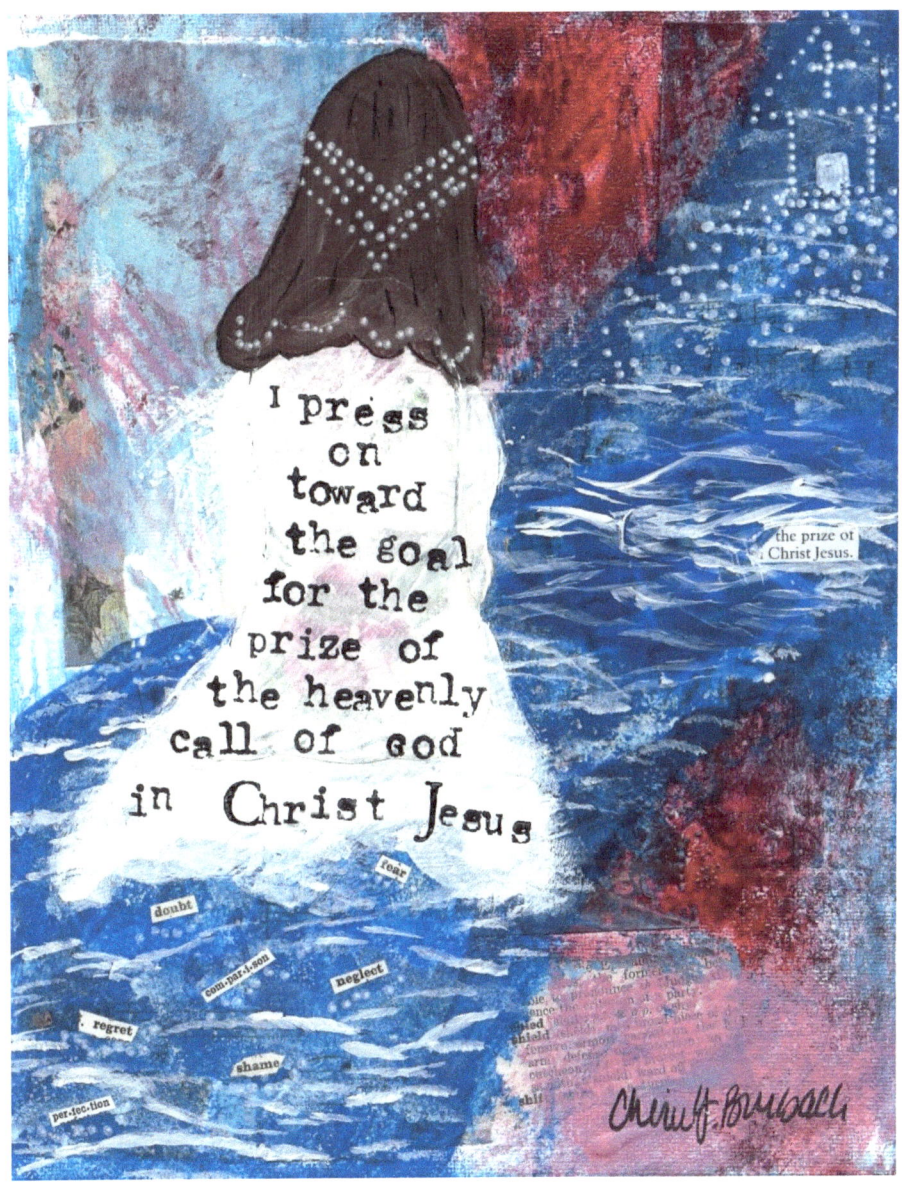

I press on toward the goal for the prize of the heavenly call of god in Christ Jesus

the prize of Christ Jesus.

doubt fear comparison neglect regret shame perfection

Fishers of Men

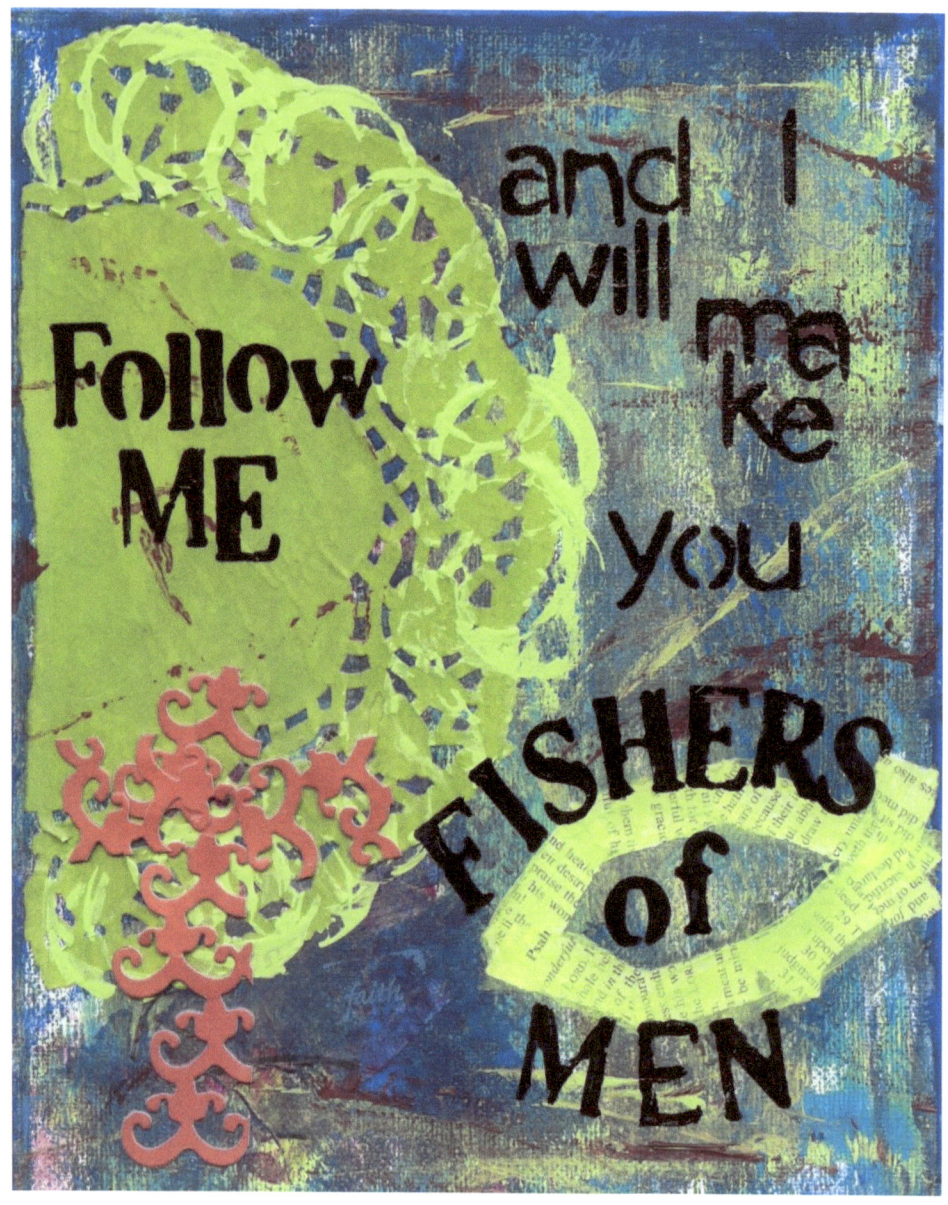

Cherie Burbach

Kingdom of Heaven

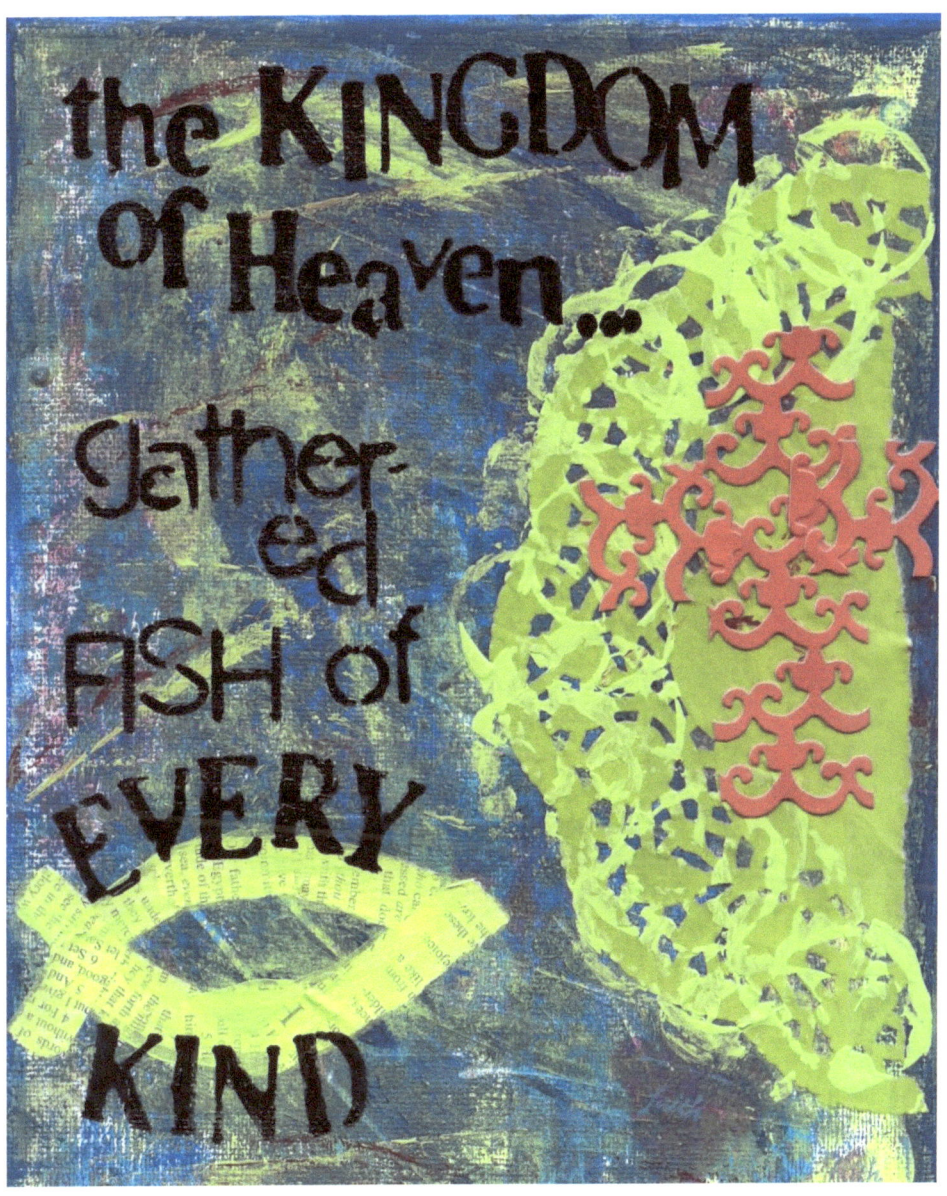

Blessed

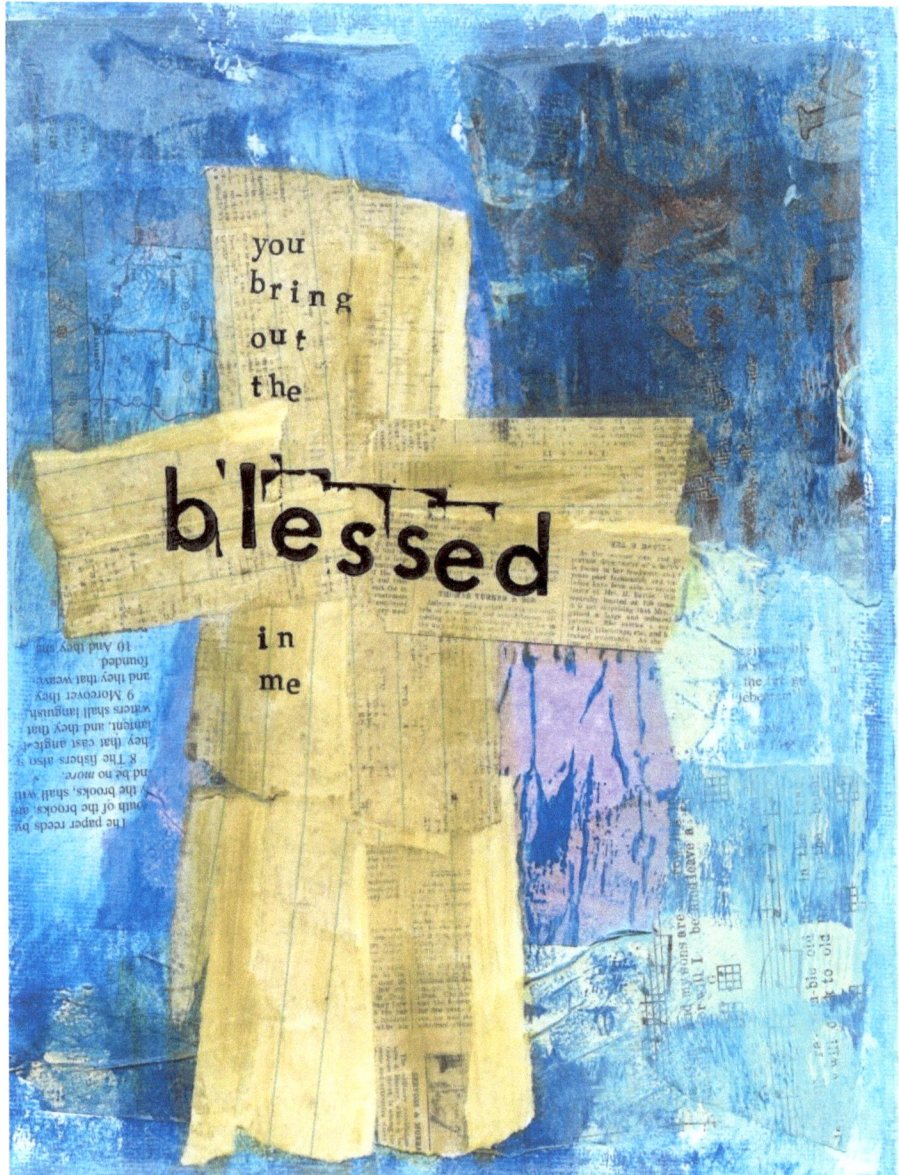

Did you ever have someone who just always reminded you about God's love? Someone who brought out the best in you? I like the thought of combining these two, and telling that person that they bring out the "blessed in you." I don't think we give this kind of compliment enough to the people who are most precious to us.

Cherie Burbach

And God Saw That the Light Was Good

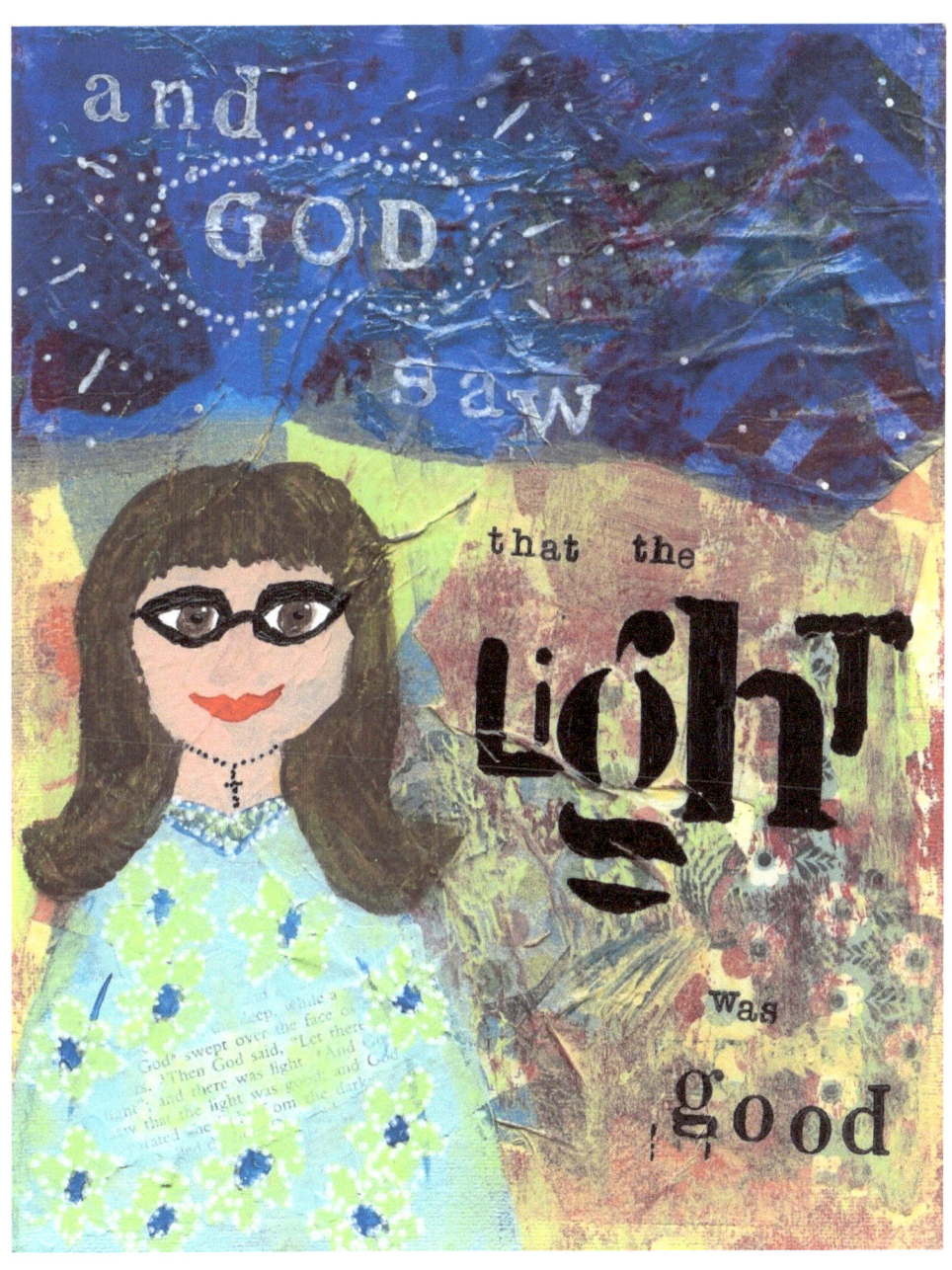

In Genesis we see how powerful God is. He creates the heavens and the earth and then the light, and we're told that He saw that *the light was good*. In Genesis 1:4 this verse continues with: *and he separated the light from the darkness*. Often the darkness in our life is scary, bleak, and something we just try to get through. But even in dark moments, there is light we can call upon to comfort us and hold us. God is always there, and He is always good.

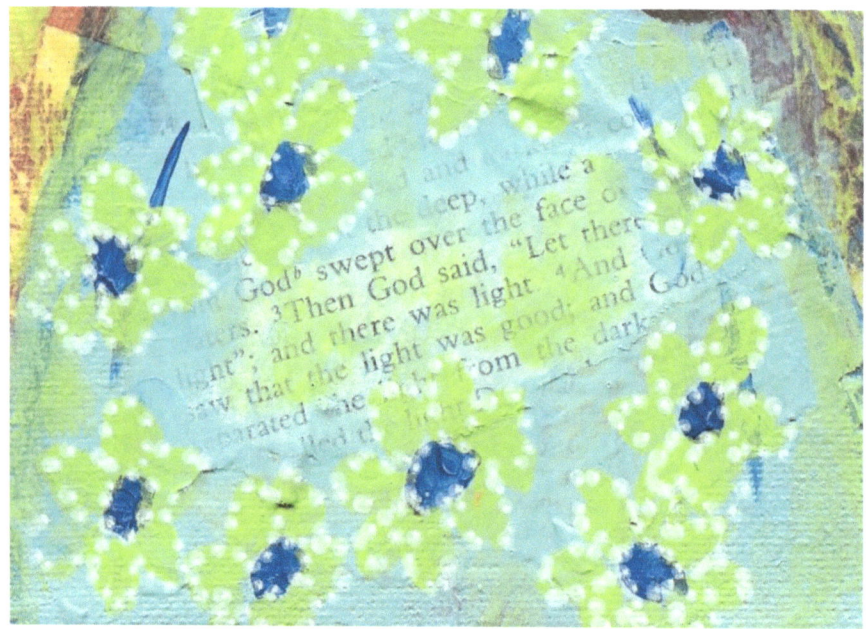

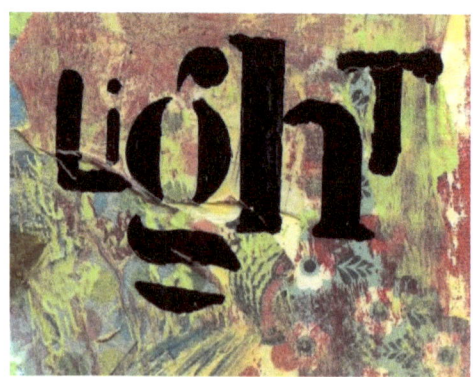

Cherie Burbach

Thou Hast Made Heaven

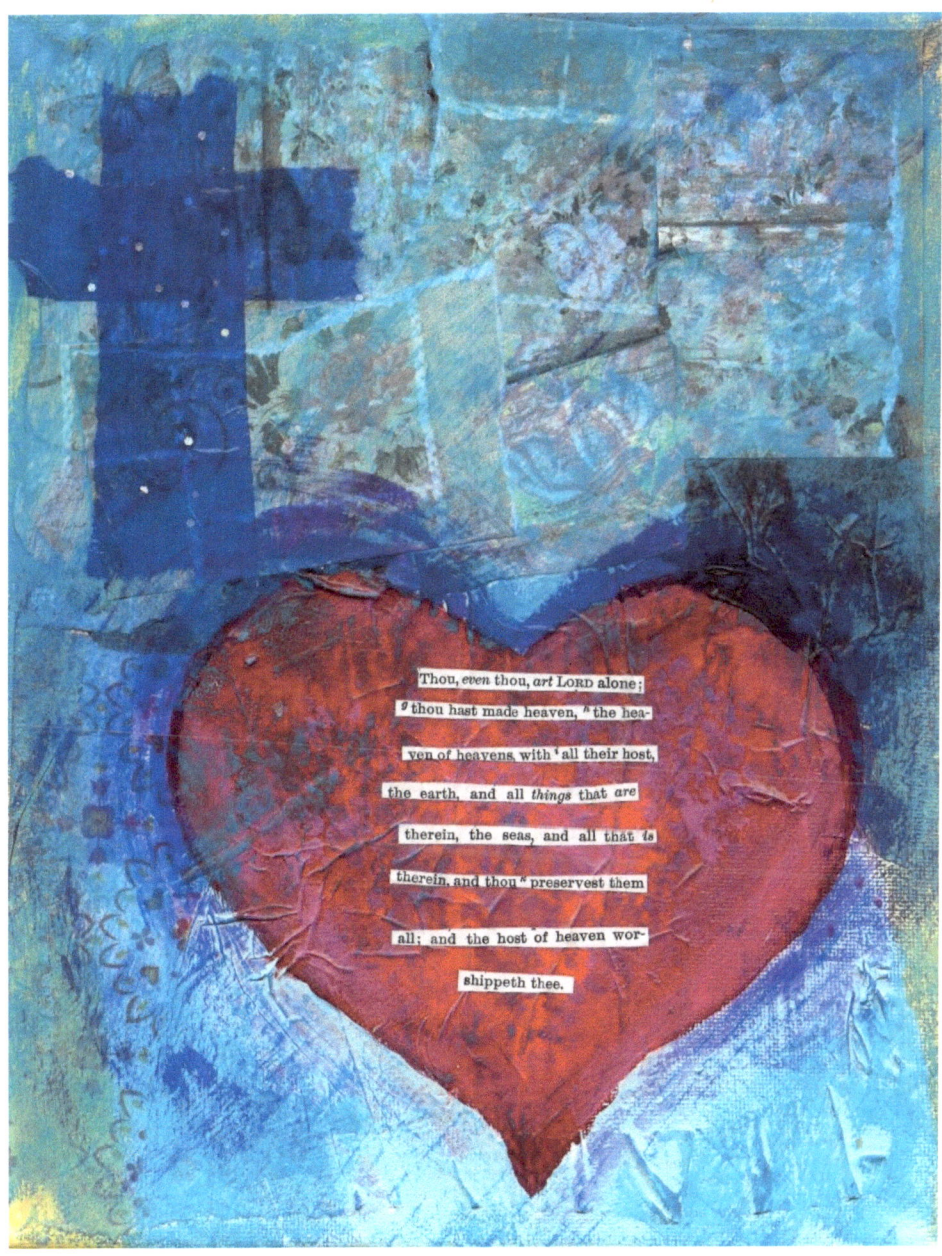

Thou, *even thou, art* LORD alone: [g] thou hast made heaven, [h] the heaven of heavens, with [i] all their host, the earth, and all *things* that *are* therein, the seas, and all that *is* therein, and thou [k] preservest them all; and the host of heaven worshippeth thee.

Beside Them the Birds of the Heavens

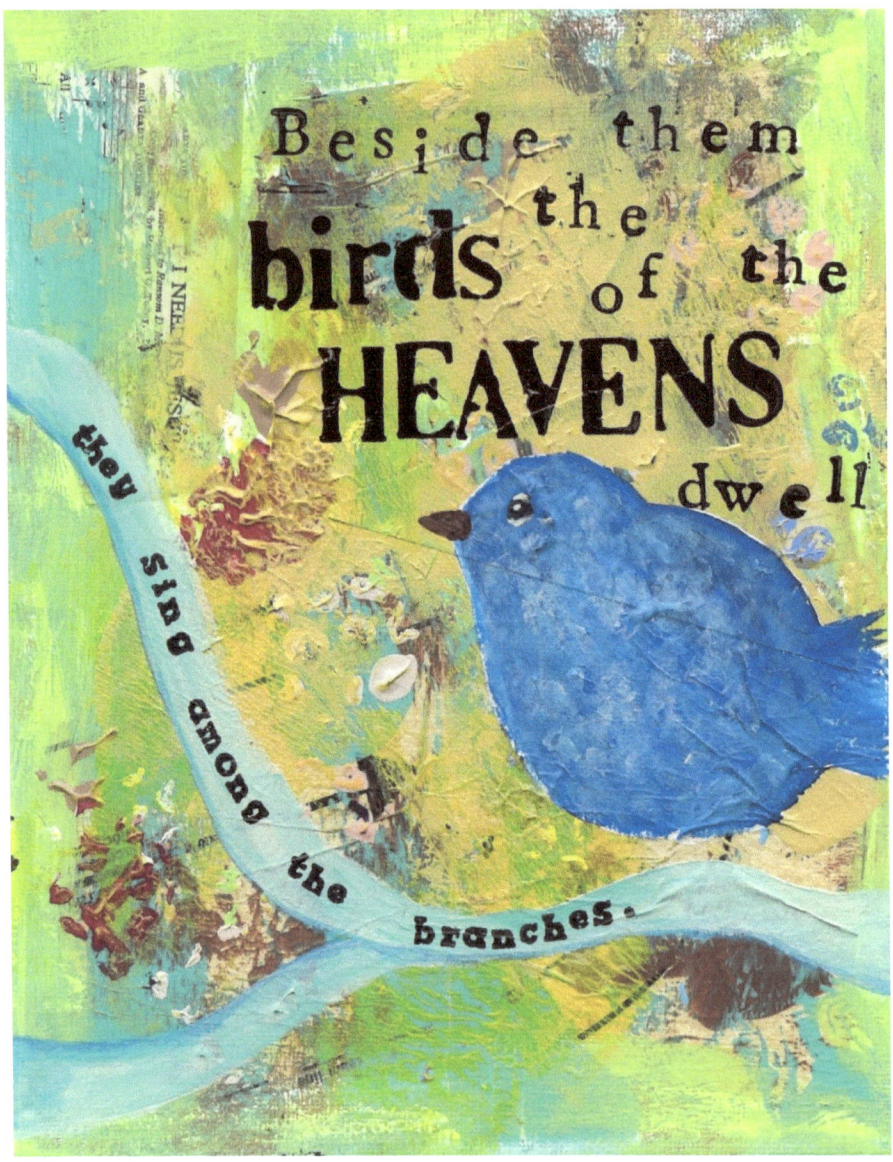

One of my favorite verses! It reminds me God's provision for our lives. He takes care of every living thing, including the smallest of birds, so fragile and light. And they honor His goodness by singing. How often do we do this? I like that this verse reminds me to never miss a moment to praise Him.

Cherie Burbach

Are You Not of More Value

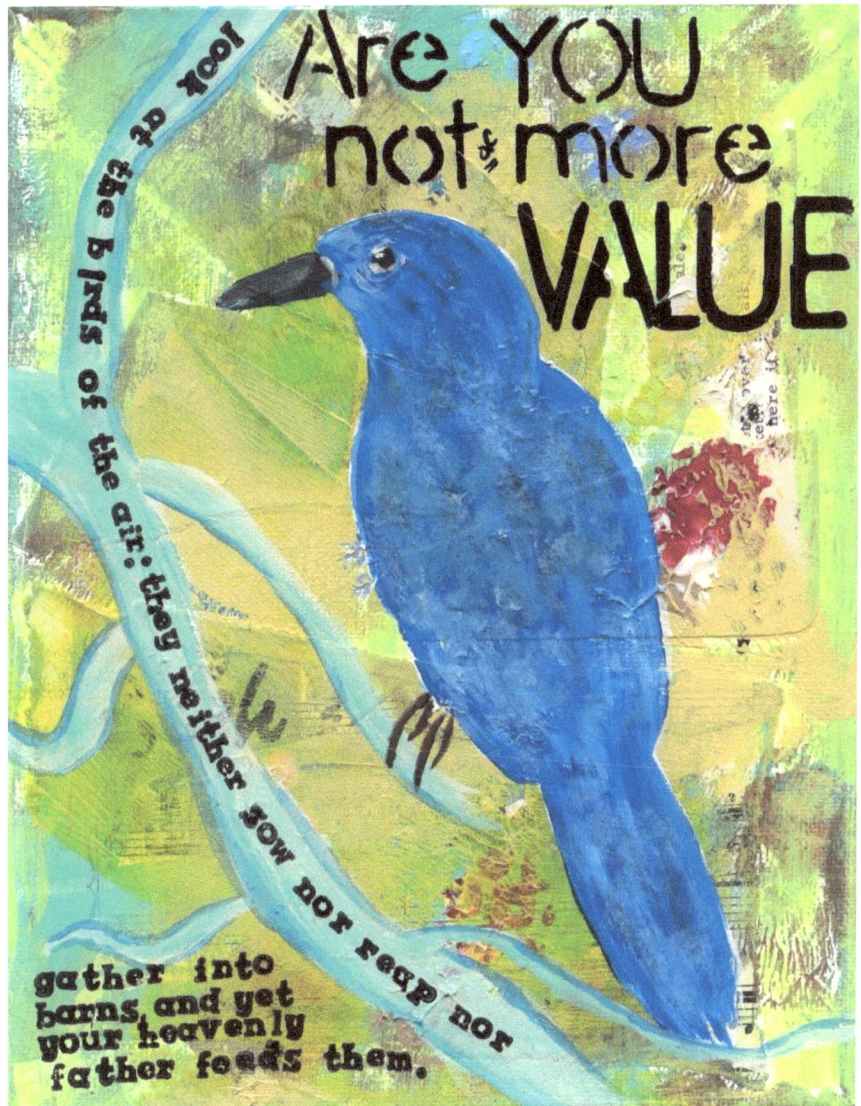

This verse, from Matthew 6:26 is another favorite since it speaks to worry. I'm still too much of a worrier, but I'm working on it. I like that this phrase is a gentle nudge to stop worrying, that God has it all under control, and yet it's also a reminder of how precious we are to Him.

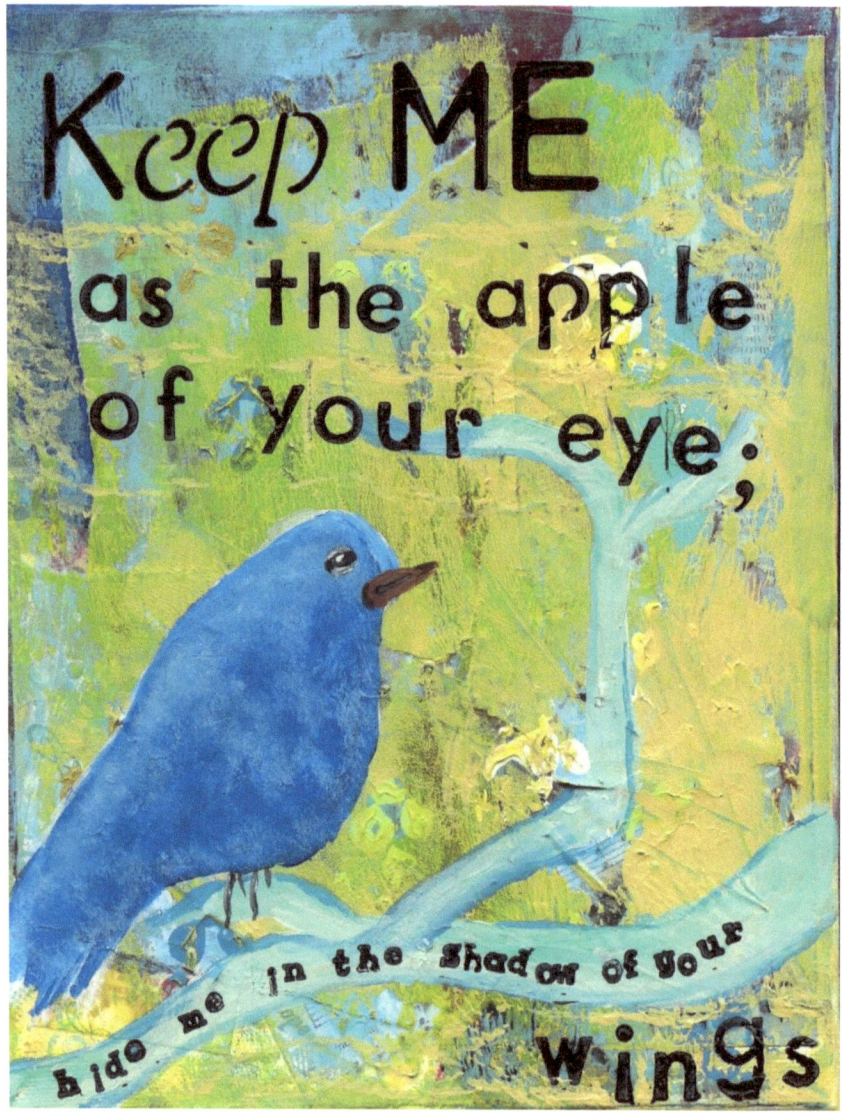

This verse, a prayer from David, requests God's protection, but also knows that he already has it. David opened up his whole self when praying to God, and he wasn't afraid to show God everything. This particular painting rounded out my "birds in branches" series, with blue birds to remind us that God's love and protection is always there.

Cherie Burbach

For Grace You Have Been Saved by Faith

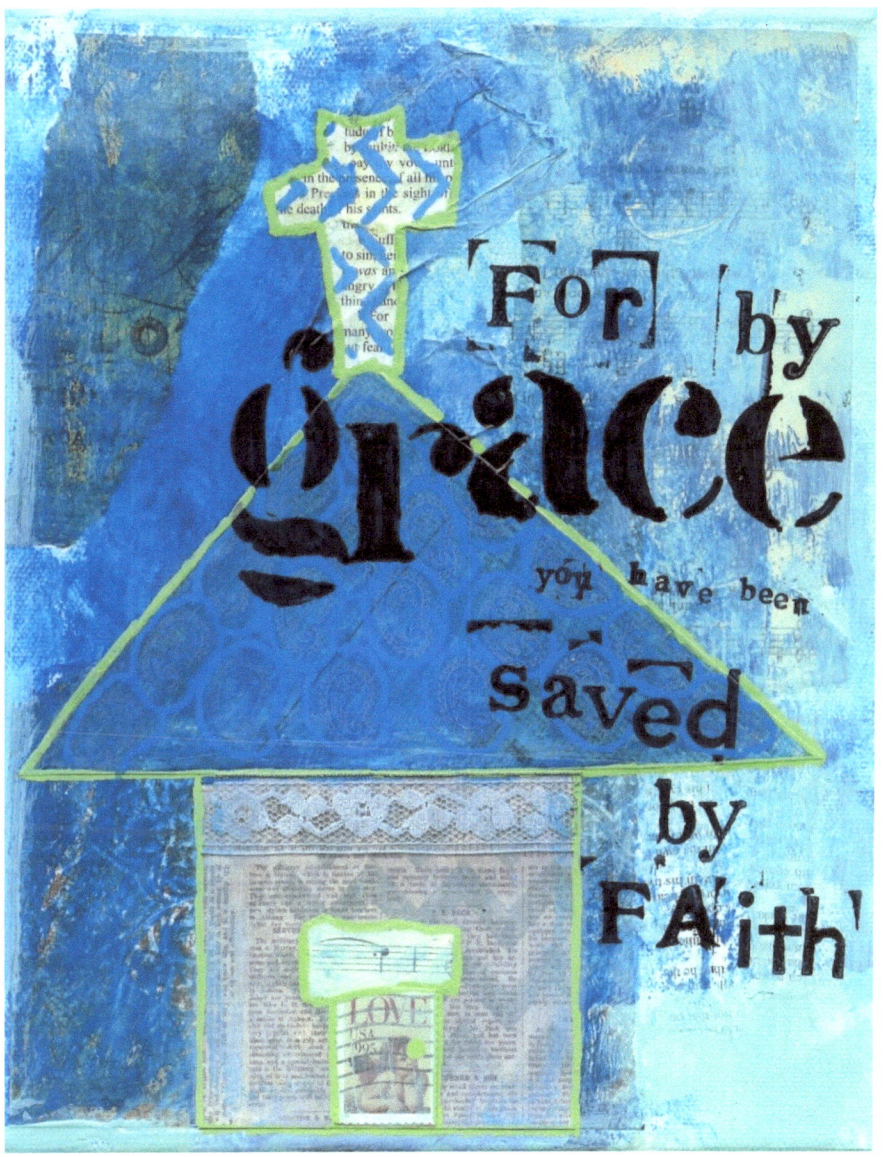

We are saved by God's grace alone. In this verse from Ephesians 2:8, we're reminded that *this is not from yourselves, it is the gift of God.*

We're saved because of Jesus, not by anything we've done. While we're encouraged to live life like Jesus did and do the good things he did, we can't buy our way into heaven. None of us deserve this grace, which reminds me once again that God loves us first so that we can love Him fully and completely.

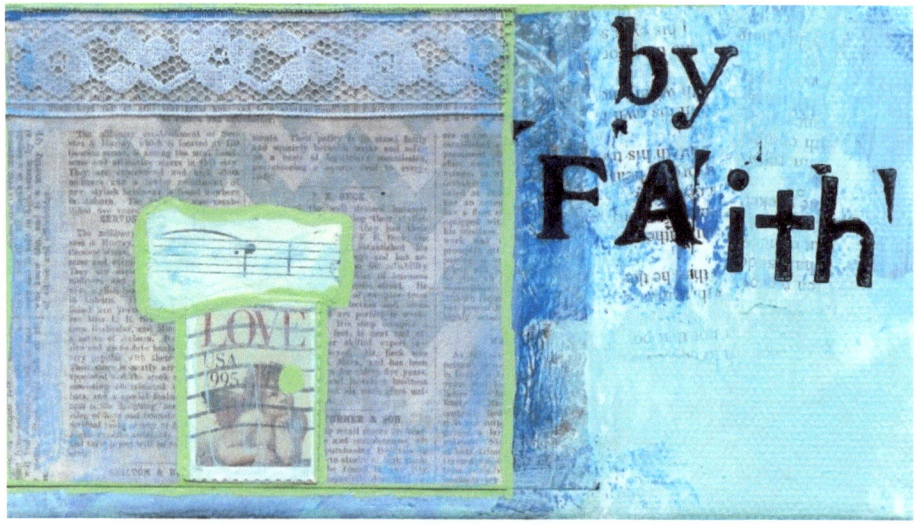

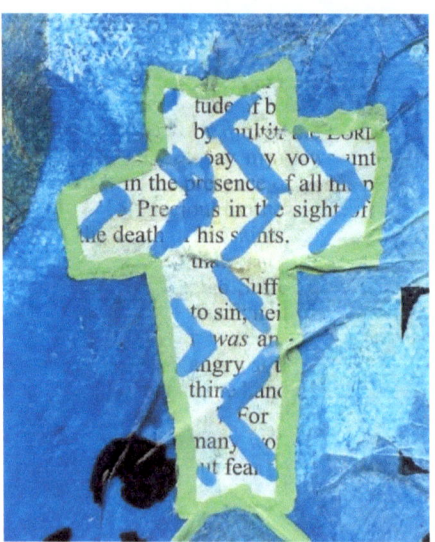

Cherie Burbach

Spread Your Wings and Soar

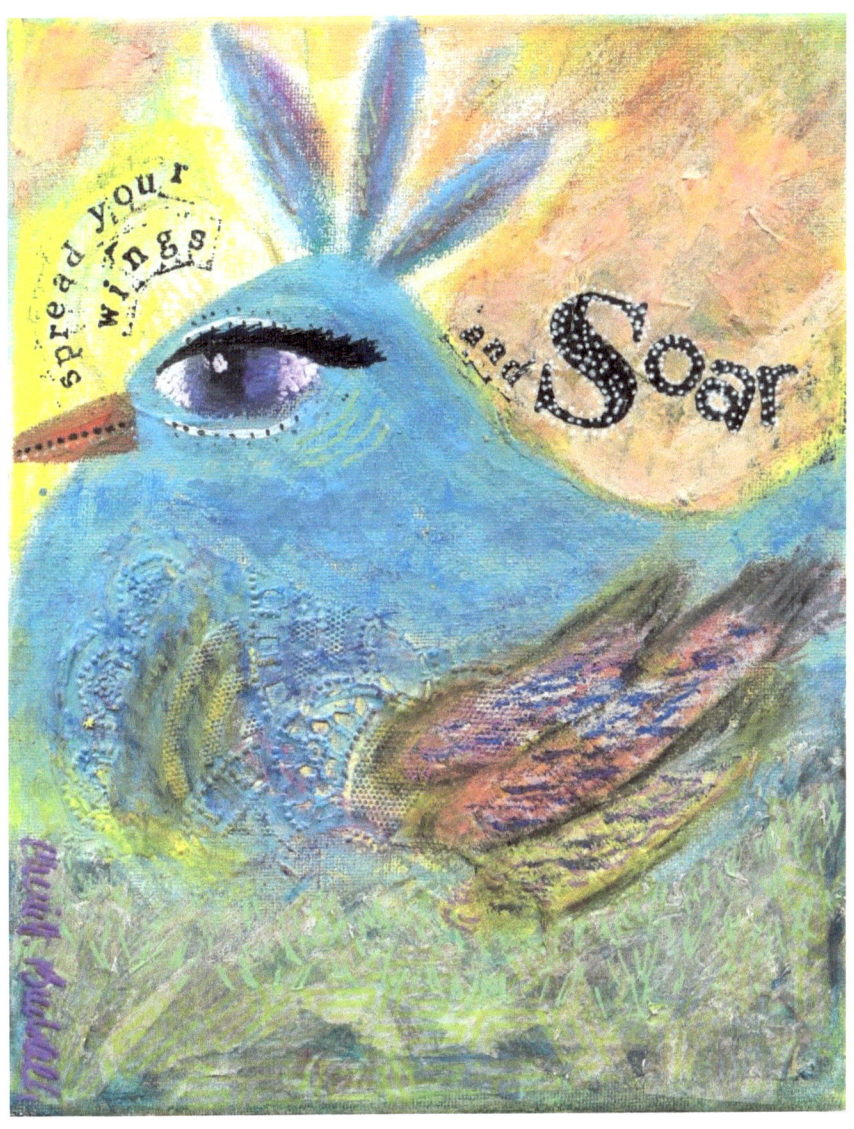

And He Said to Them

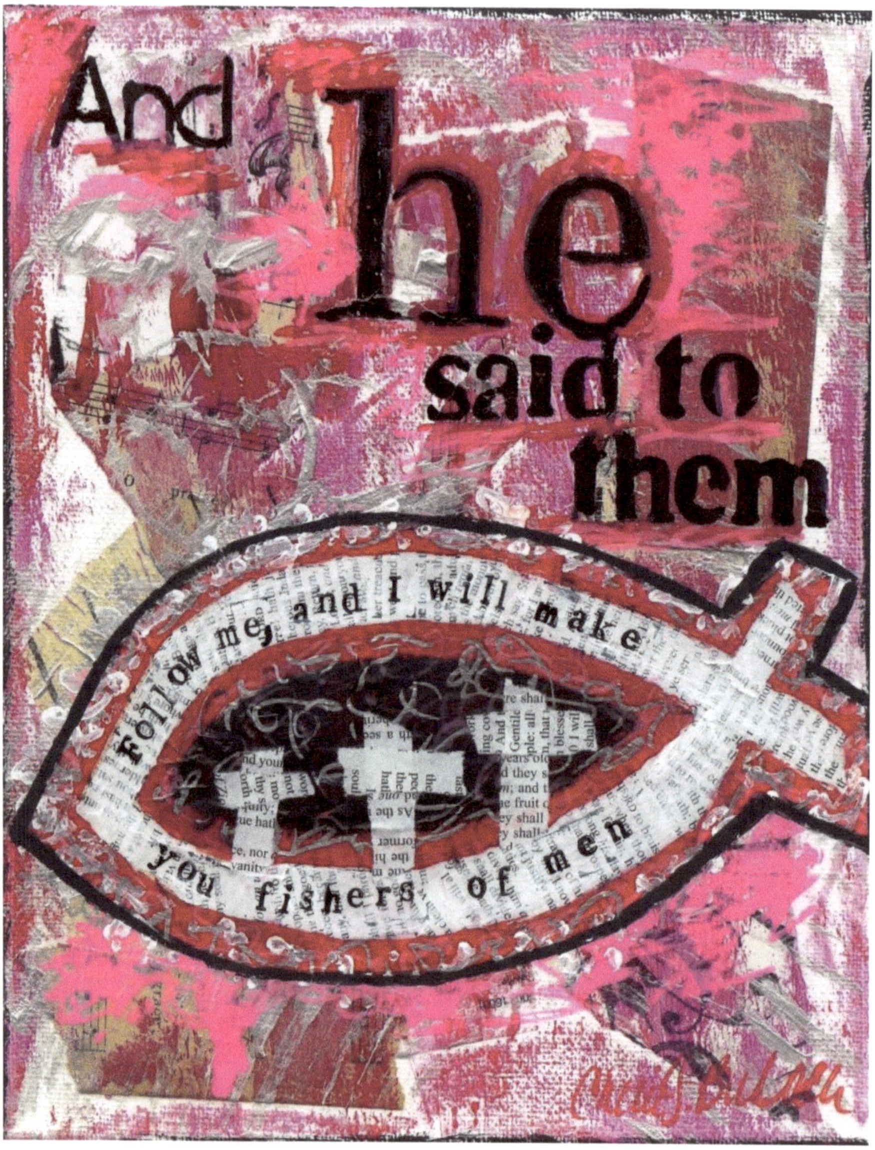
And
he
said to
them
Follow me, and I will make
you fishers of men

Fish of Every Kind

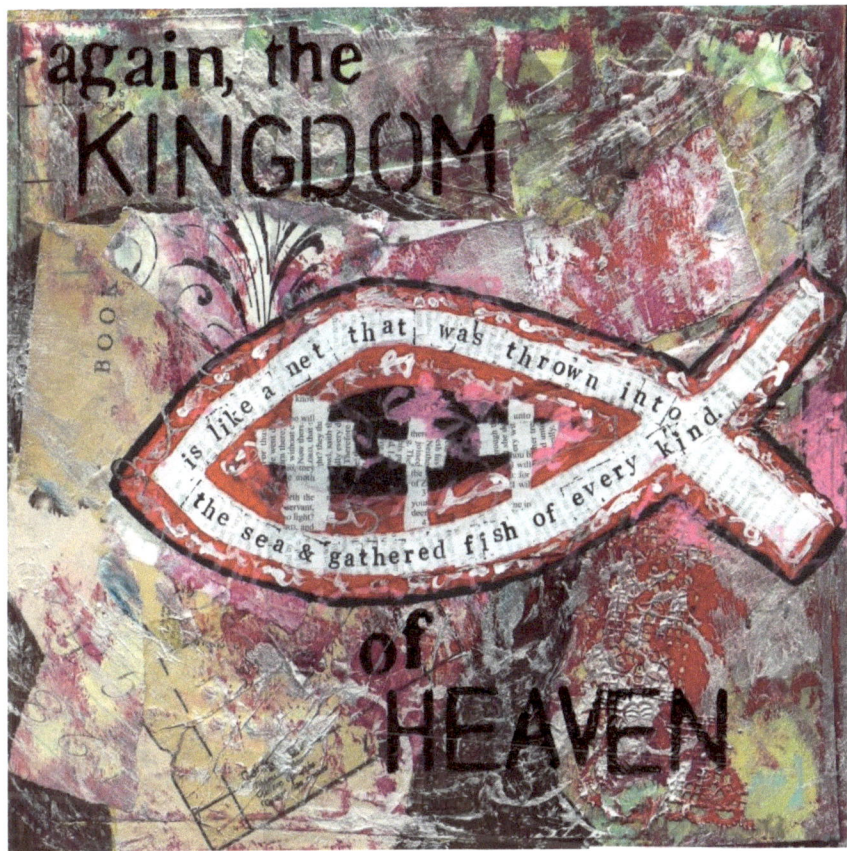

This series began with a desire to shift the color palette I normally work with. I added more pinks and reds and even experimented with silver. I wanted to show how the "messiness" of life is still ordered and beautiful when God is in control. You see things differently when you trust Him. Too often, we look at life too closely without knowing that there is a big picture at work. We see the disappointments up close and they look ugly and sad, but if we could step back and see them from a distance, they might look exactly like they belong, highlighting the good times to make them stand out even brighter.

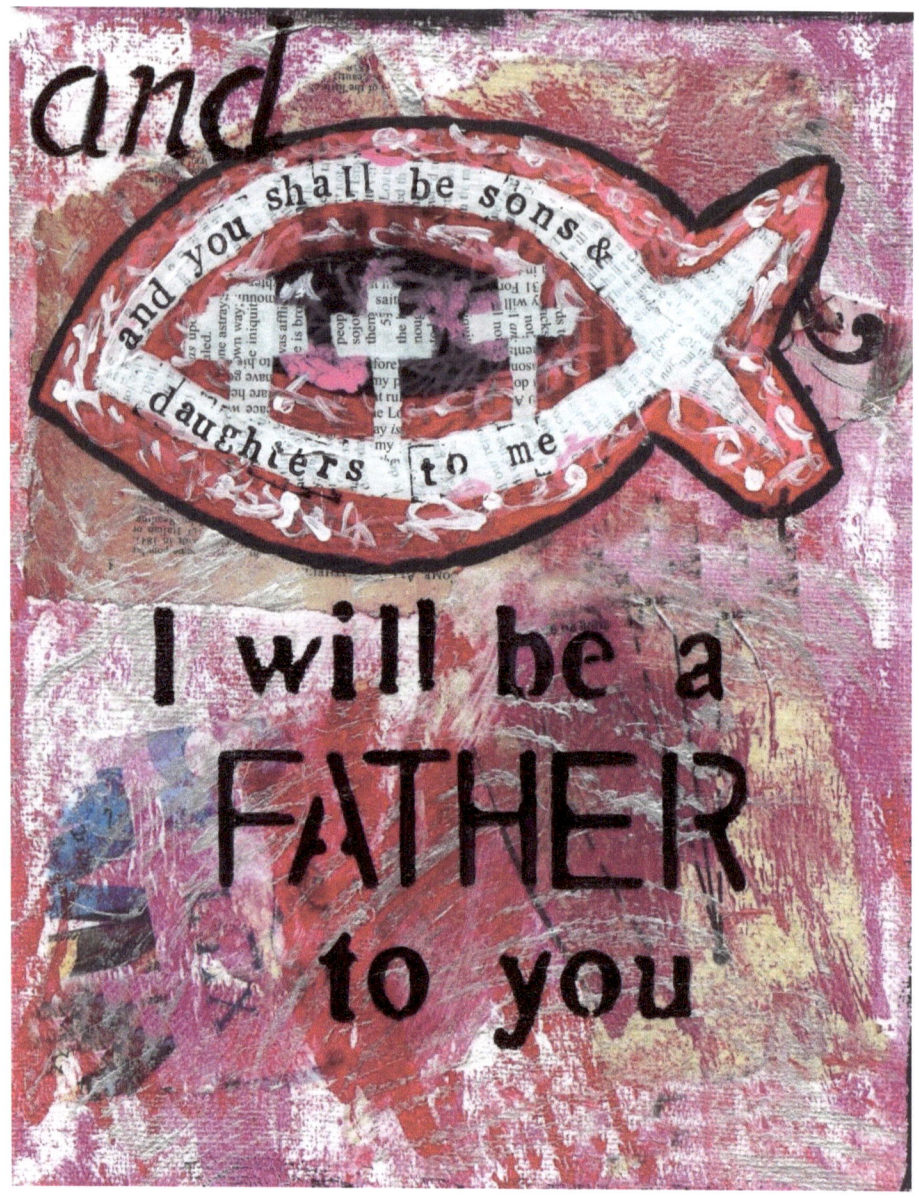

Cherie Burbach

I Can Do All Things

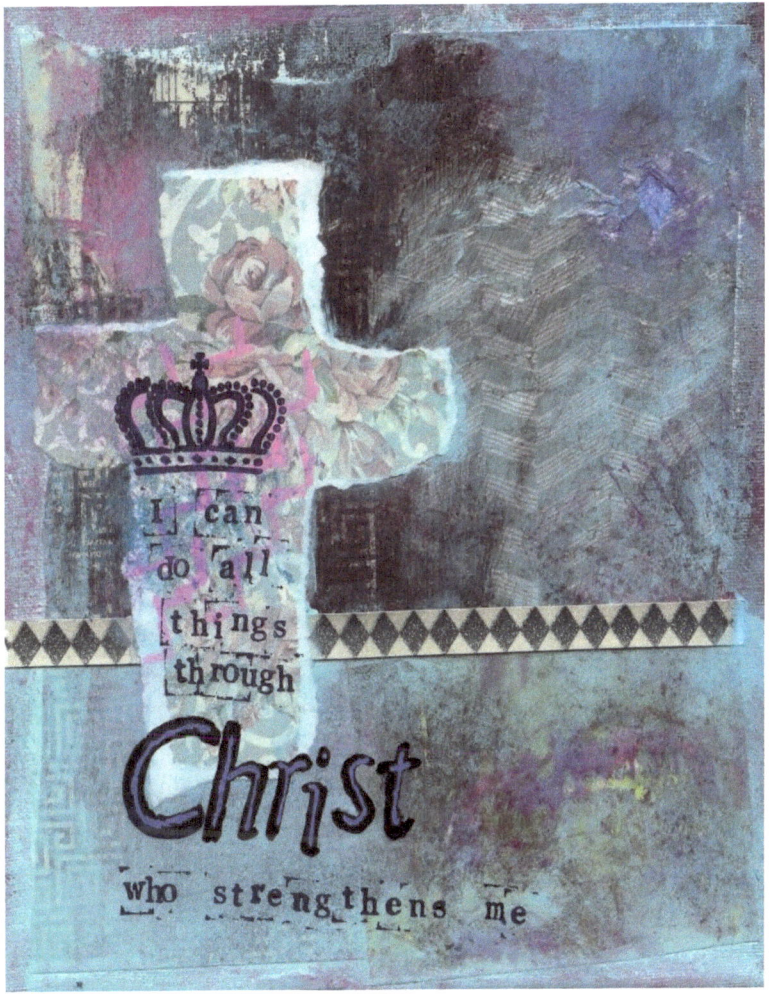

There are times when we feel weak, and need to remember this verse, that God is there for us and strengthens us always.

But there are also times when we're feeling great, so much so that maybe we aren't thinking about needing God so much. This is also the time to think about these words from Philippians 4:13, because He is the one in control, even when we feel like we are.

Put on the Full Armor of God

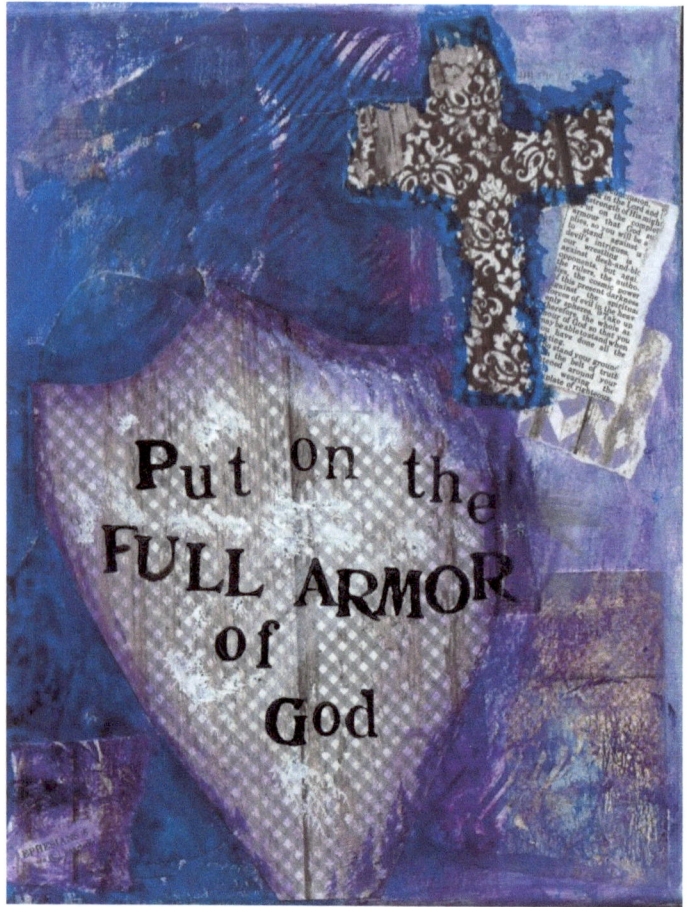

In Ephesians 6:11 we are reminded of God's strength again, this time as our protection. To me, this means a lot of prayer. The world is such a distracting place. Too many images in the news and pop culture to distract us, too many ways to spend our free time with games and the Internet and TV, and to really put on the armor of God I need to first quiet myself so I can talk with Him and listen. If I feel I need protection, I ask for it, even though I know He is already there. But it's my hope that in this busy world I can always hear His voice above all others, including my own.

Cherie Burbach

Path of Life

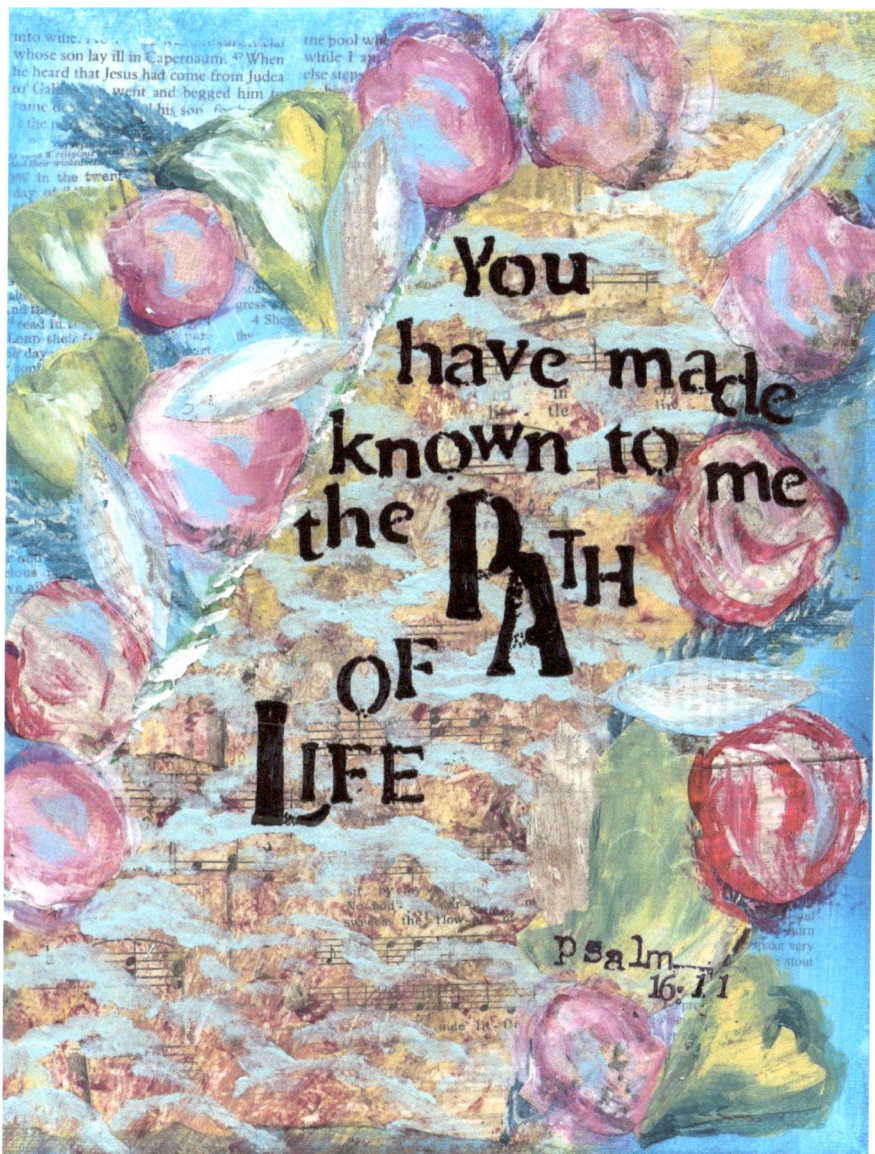

This verse, from Psalm 16:11, talks of joy in the presence of God now and for eternity. The path of life is a long, secure one with God, not just for this world but for the next one as well.

The Lord Is My Shepherd, I Shall Not Want

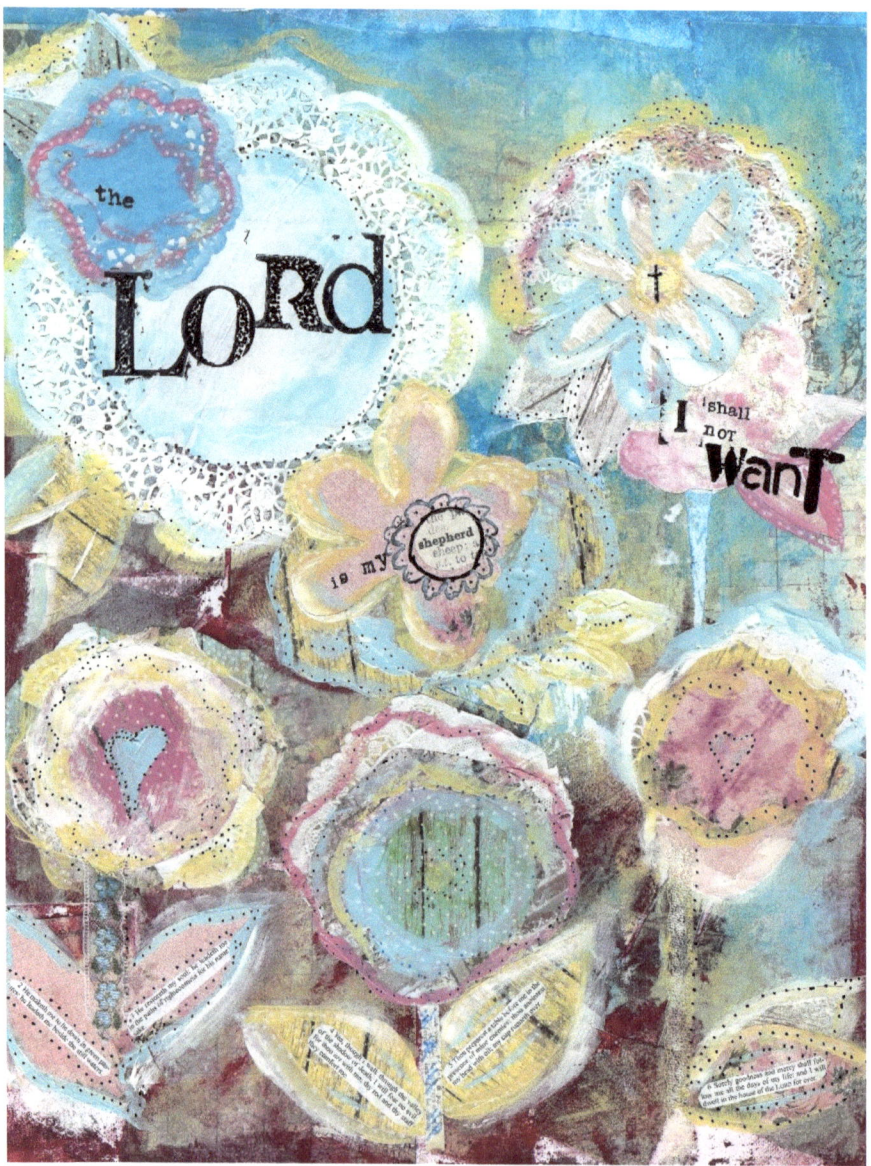

The Lord is my shepherd, I shall not want. There is a reason the 23rd Psalm is such a popular verse with people. The poetry of this verse speaks to the ultimate truth that God will care for us, no matter what is going on. He's there, leading us, providing for our needs.

Cherie Burbach

You Give Life

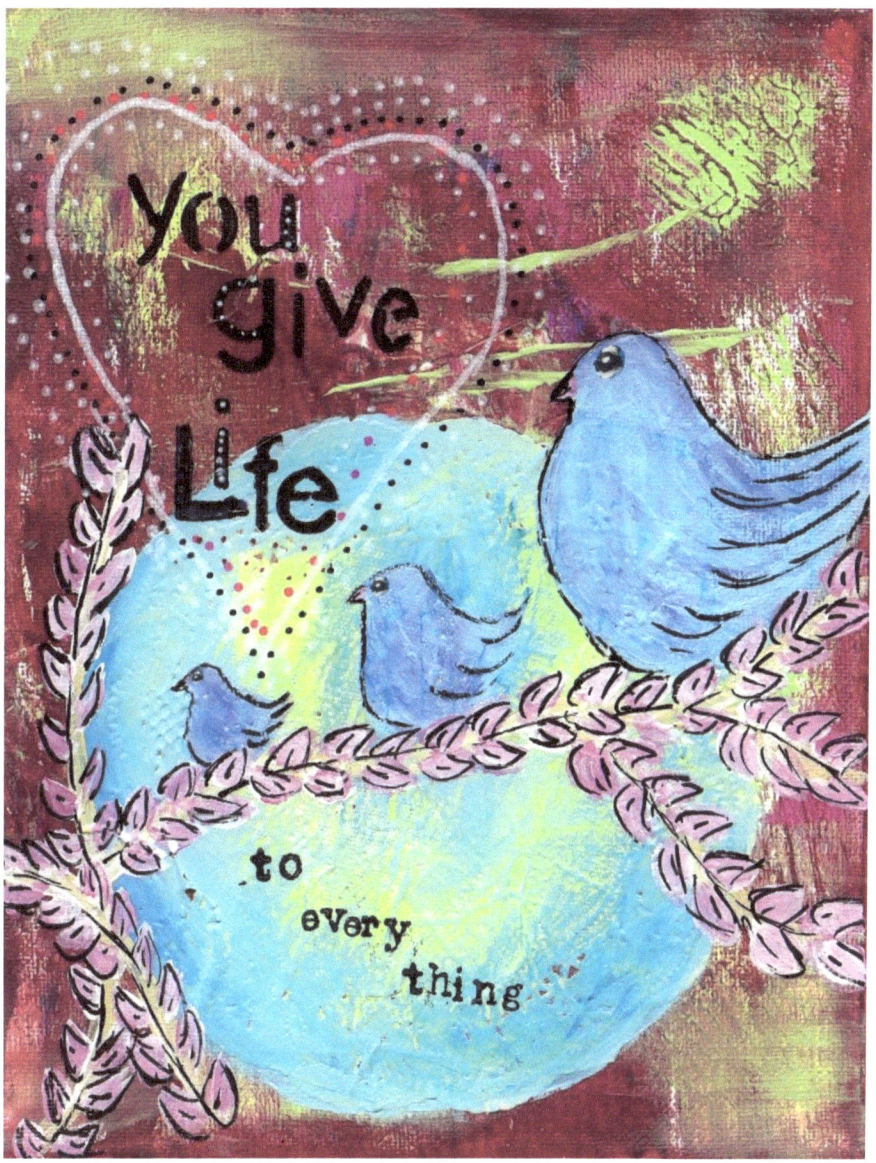

I like the ending of this verse from Nehemiah 9:6: *and the multitudes of heaven worship you.*

He Restores My Soul

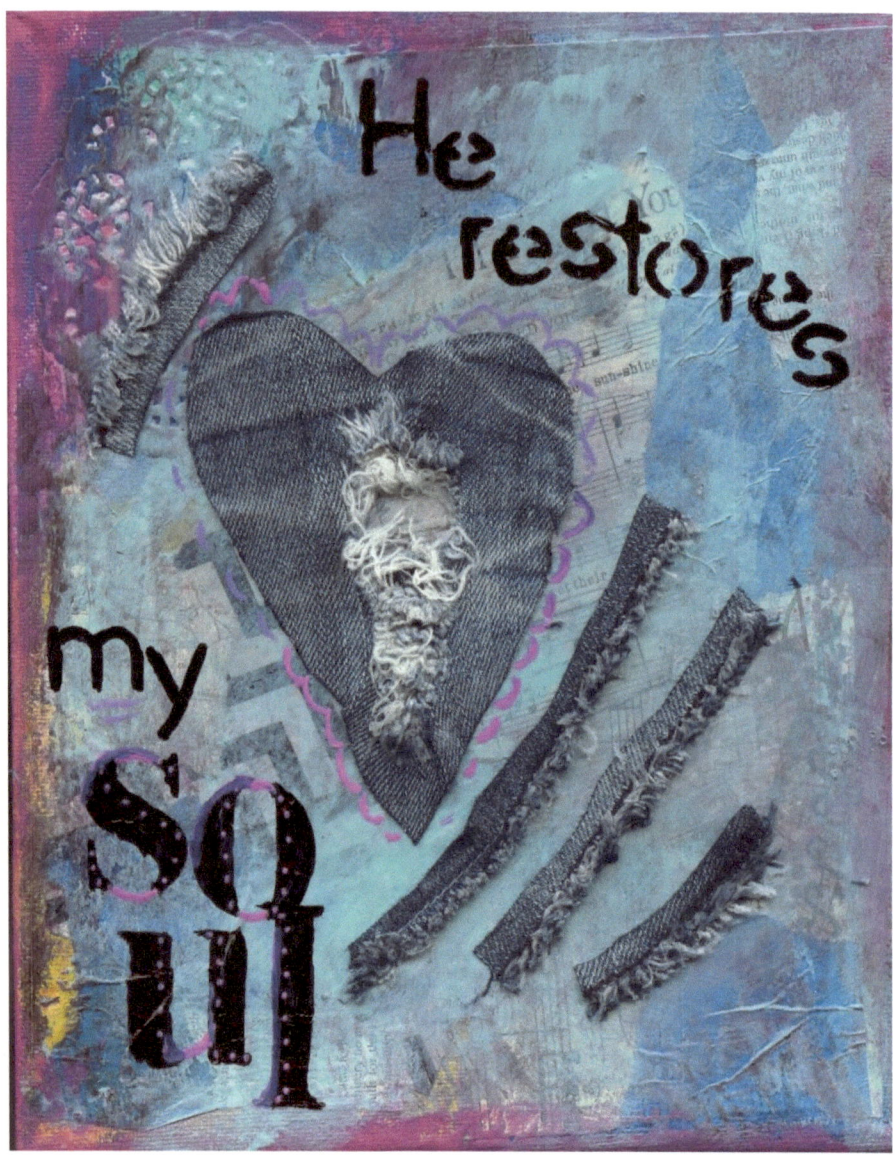

I'm finding this verse more and more true as I get older. Only time alone with God can really restore my spirit and help me feel centered again. I find it when I'm painting or writing poetry, or just quietly praying at the start of the day.

Cherie Burbach

I Lift Up My Soul

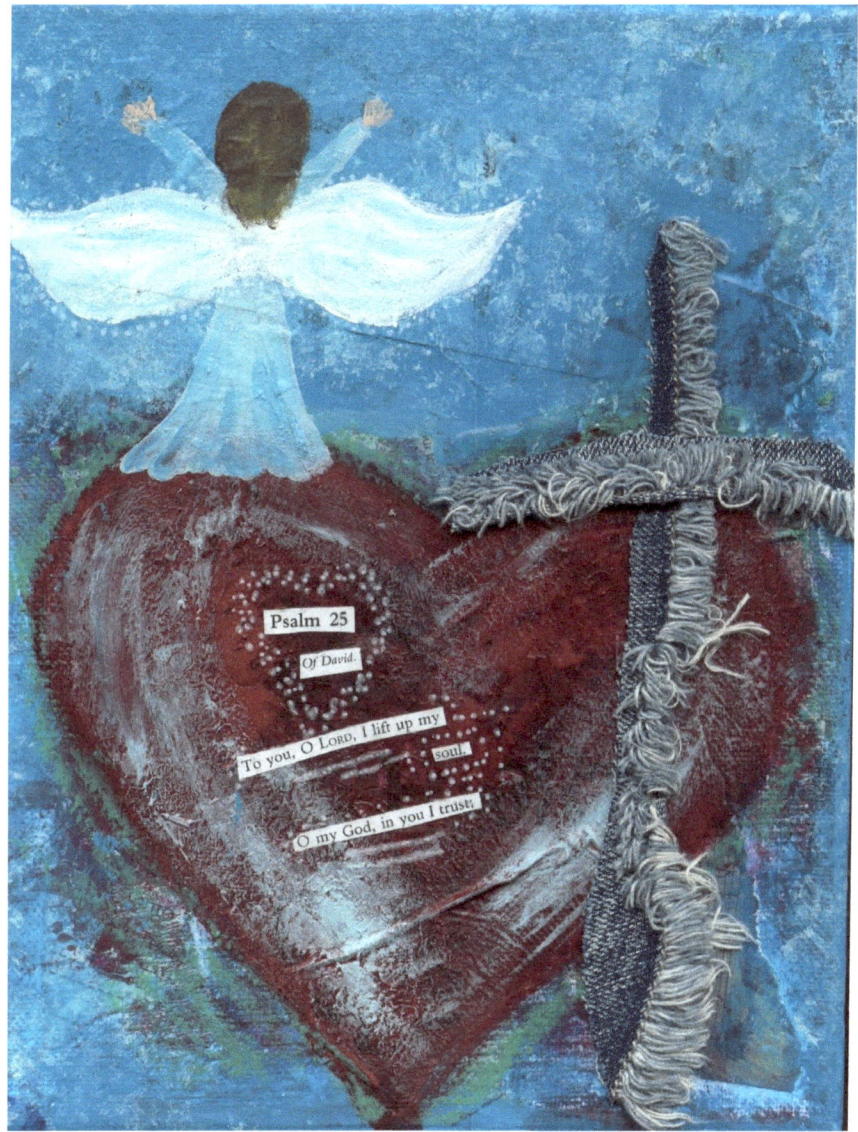

In 2016 I adopted the word "trust" as my theme for the year, and this verse sums up my desire perfectly: O my God, in you I trust. There are times when I need this reminder, when I start questioning why things are happening to me, and this verse brings me back to where I need to be: *just trust.*

In Him Was Life

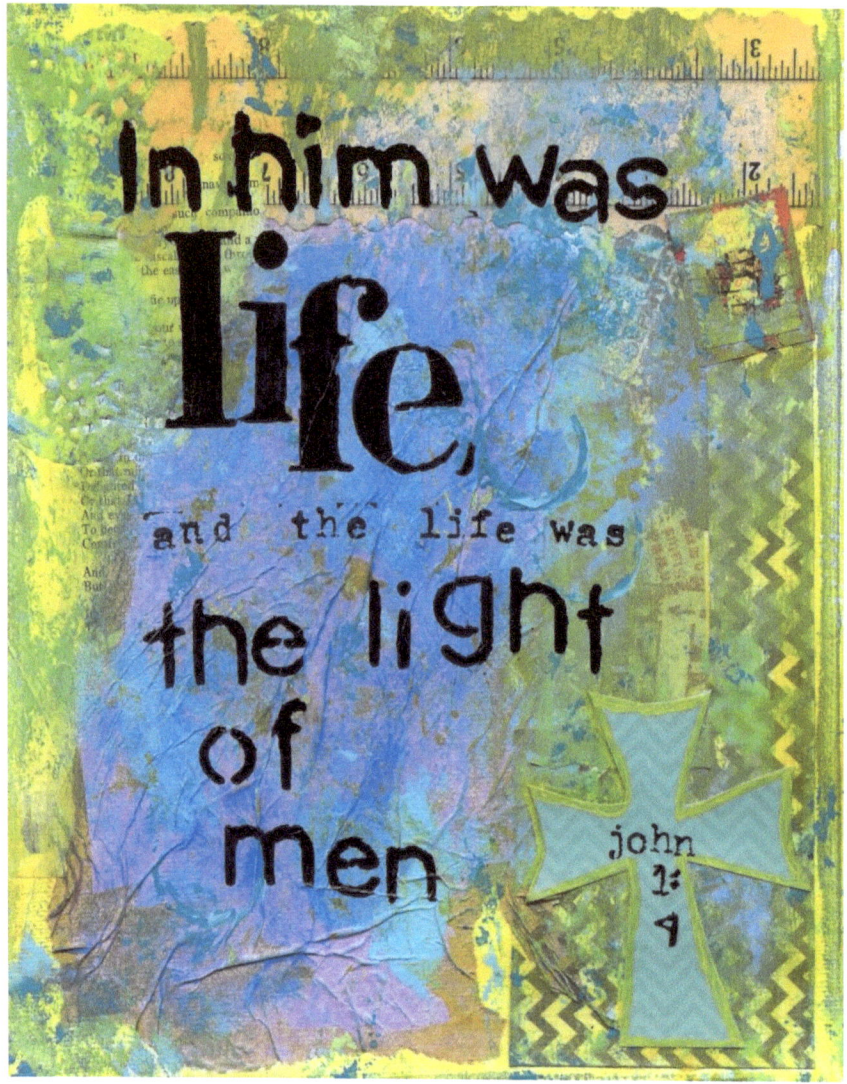

The gospel of John is like poetry and often shows me what God's love is all about in a different way than the other gospels do. He has a way of phrasing things that sings to my soul!

Cherie Burbach

The Fruit of the Spirit

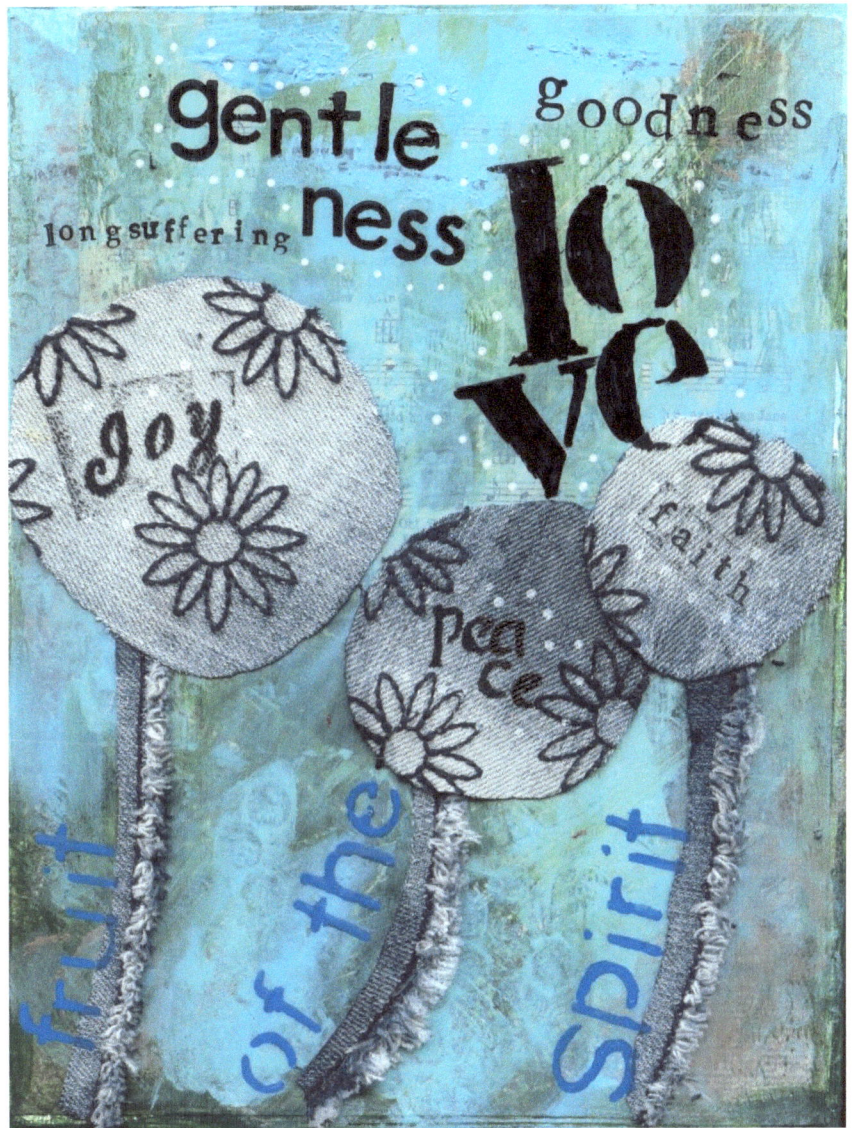

It seems that when we're learning about God and how to act as a follower of His should, we often hear about the things we shouldn't do. It's important to establish these guidelines. But we can't forget the good things that come from being followers as well, and these signs can help us stay on track and encourage us.

John 3:16

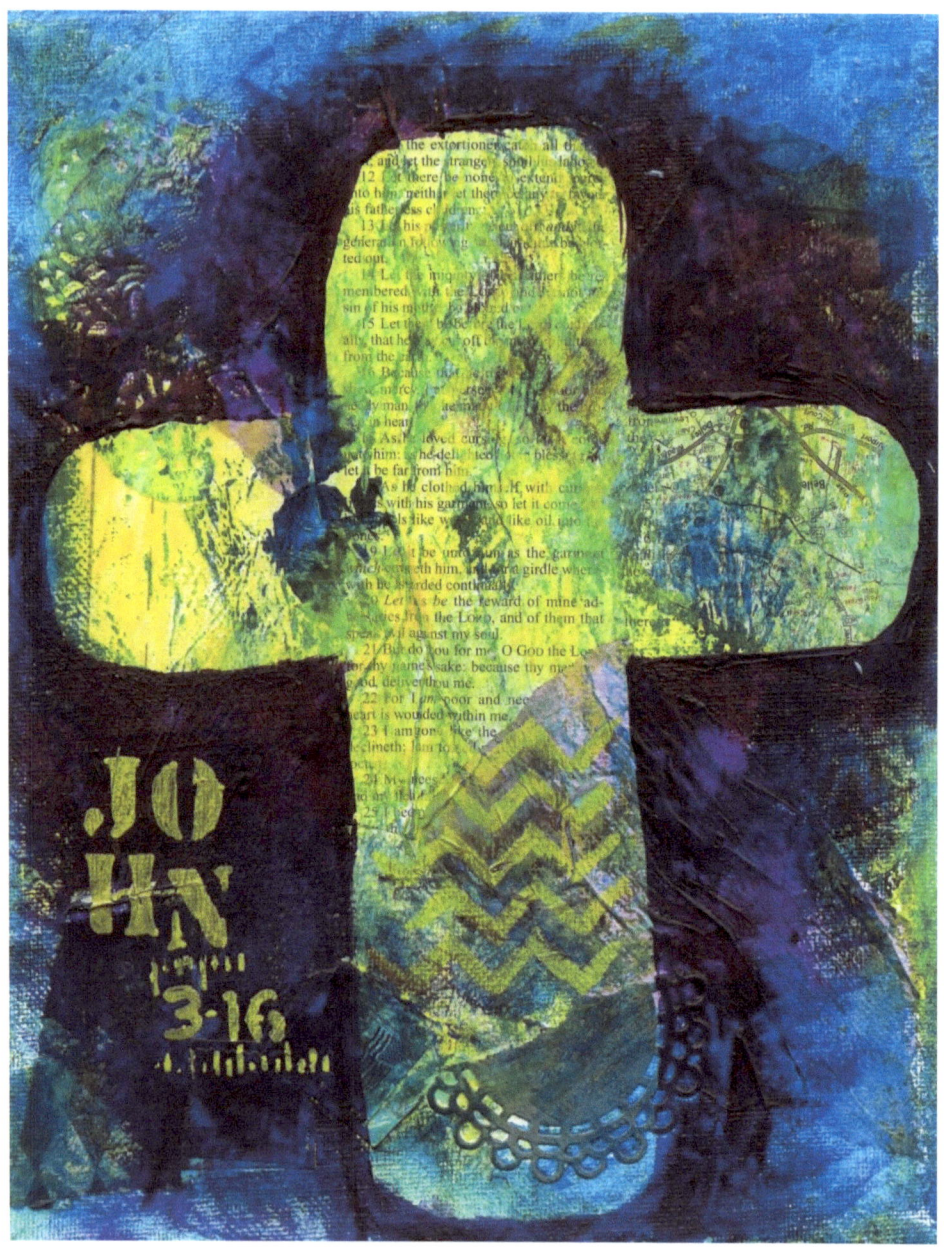

Cherie Burbach

Clothe Yourselves in Compassion

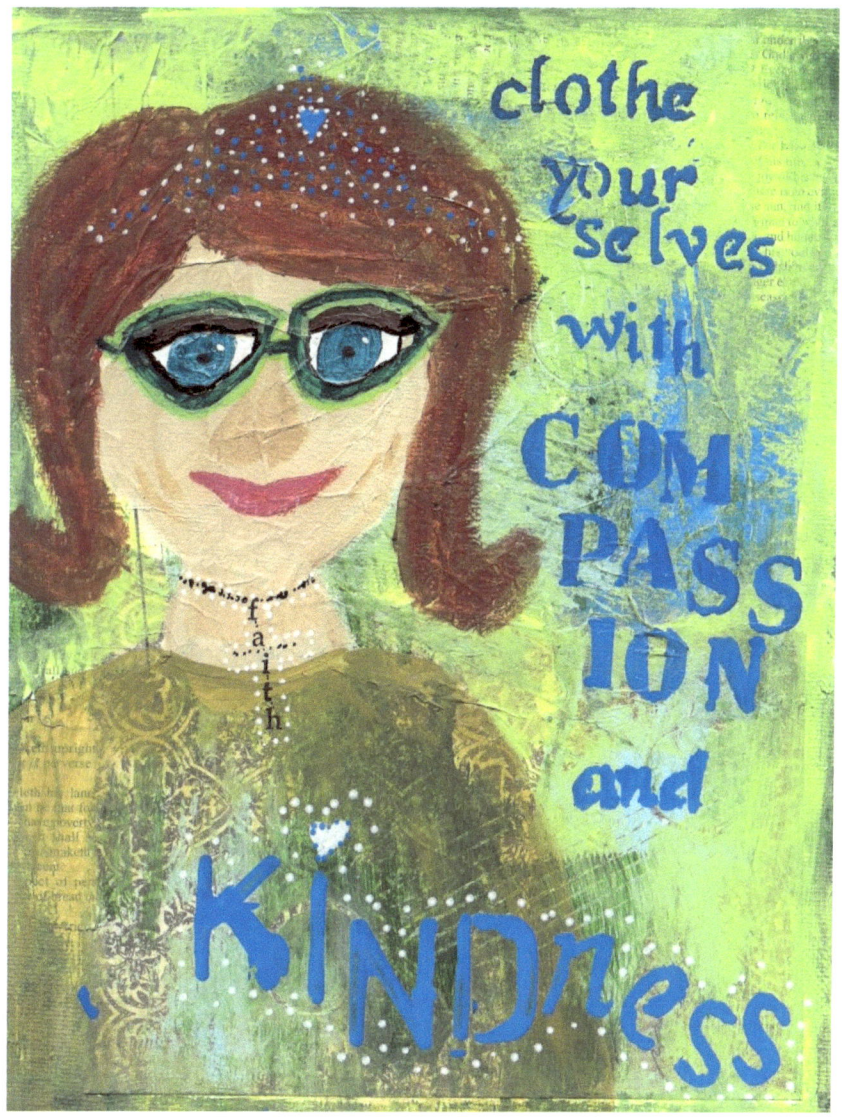

To actively live in peace you have to be kind. God reminds us of this. I like the thought of wrapping kindness around us, so that people see it when we walk in a room like they would a colorful scarf or finely made sweater. Let people see your outward kindness so they can come closer and learn of your inner joy with God.

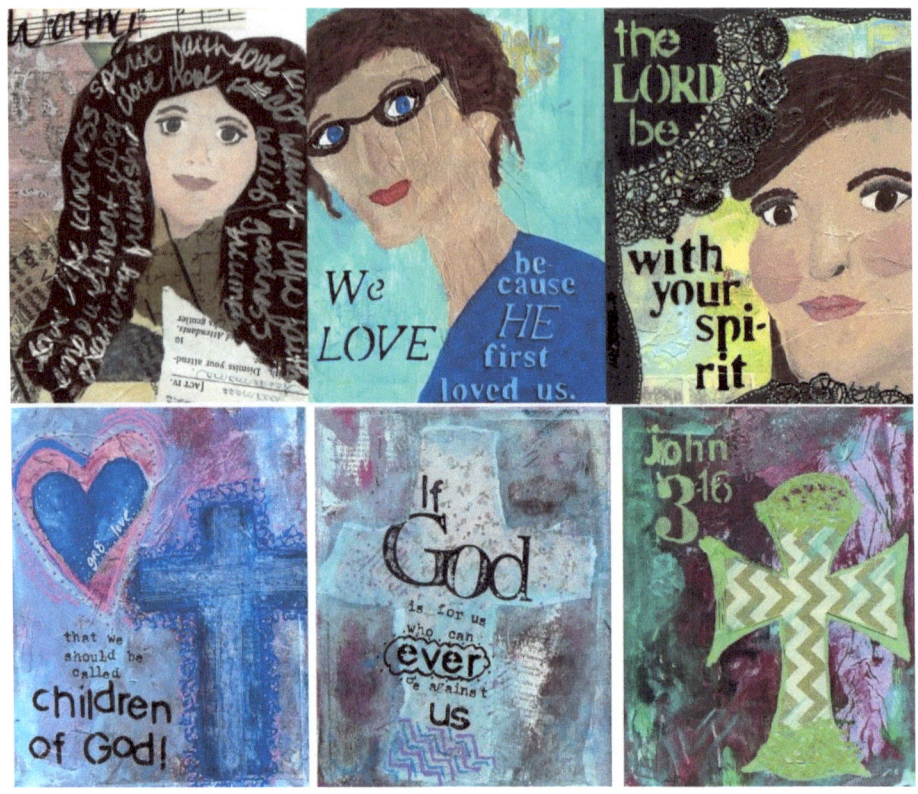

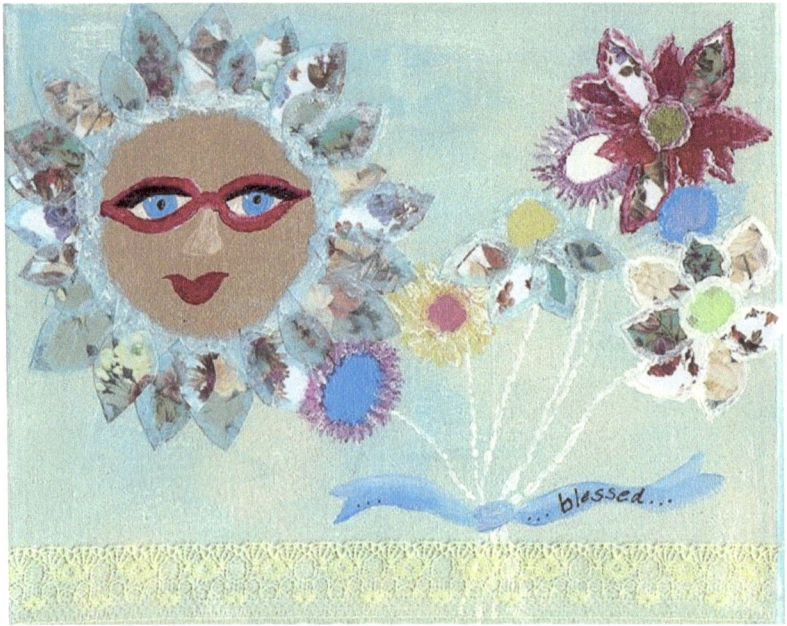

Cherie Burbach

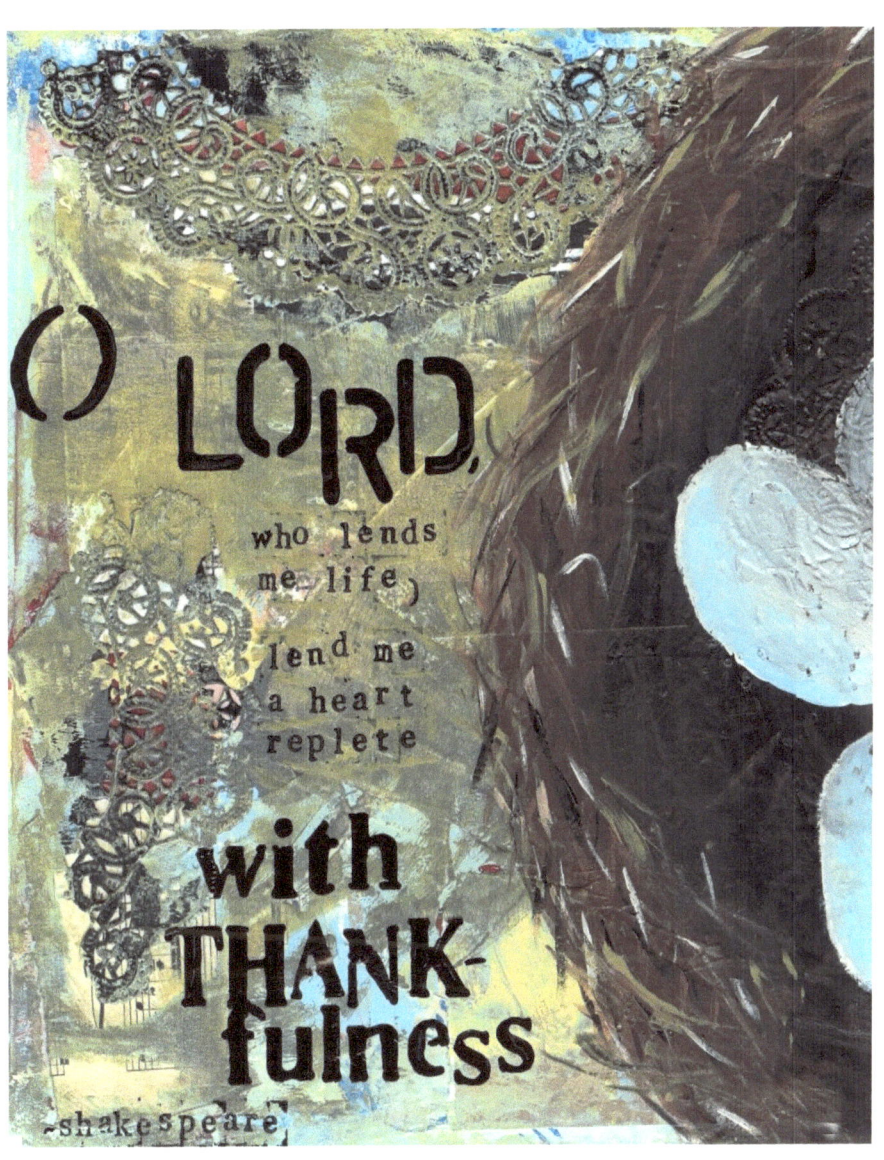

O LORD,

who lends
me life,
lend me
a heart
replete

with
THANK-
fulness

-shakespeare

Using Your Creative Gifts

If you read my blog you've probably heard me say "use your creative gifts." Your creative gifts don't have to be perfect (in fact, it's better if they aren't!), they don't have to be like anyone else's (again, better if they're not) and they don't have to be something huge. While it's great to work as a writer or artist, it doesn't mean that if you're not in those professions you can't be creative.

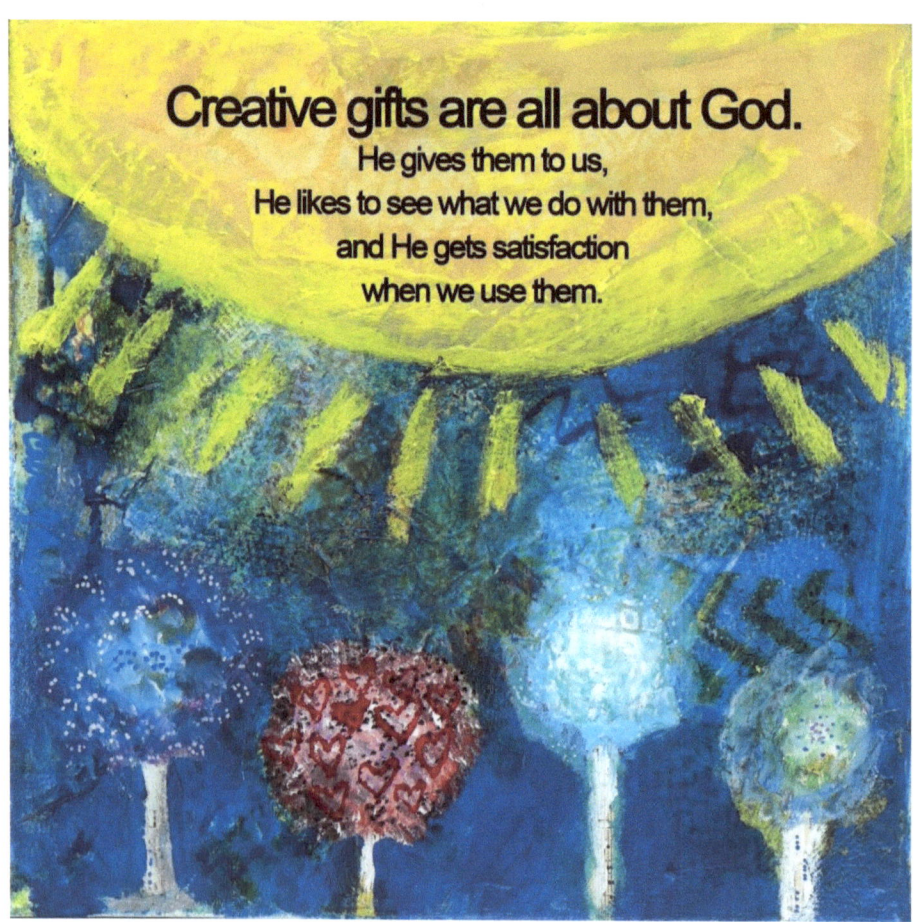

Cherie Burbach

The term creative gifts comes from my aunt, who has told me this time and time again over the years. If I'd call and talk about my day at work, she'd say, "But are you making time for your creative gifts?" If I complained about a failed relationship, she'd tell me to work it out using my creative gifts.

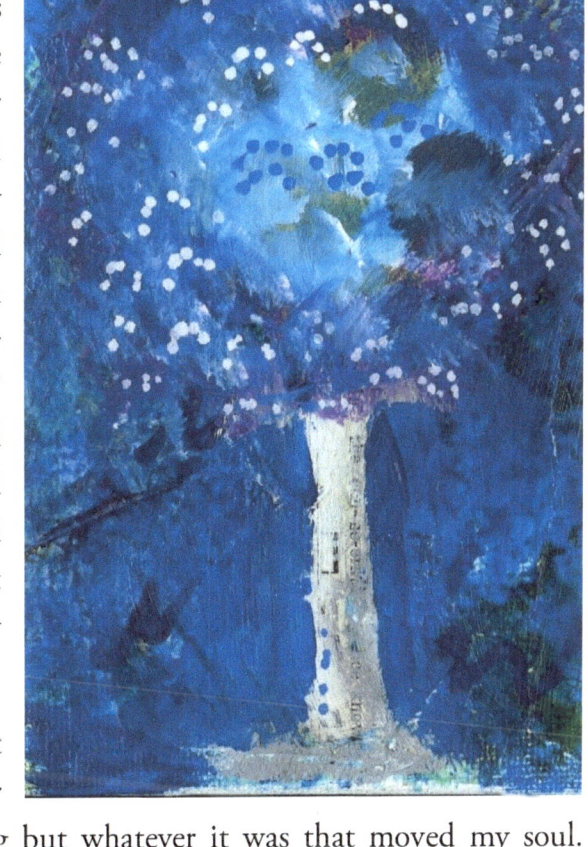

She didn't just mean writing or painting or crafting but whatever it was that moved my soul. Creative gifts are all about God. He gives them to us, He likes to see what we do with them, and He gets satisfaction when we use them. Believe it! If I go a week where I haven't used them in some way, I feel bad. This is important, because my normal mode is *work work work*. I love working, and have a hard time walking away. But being creative uses a different vibe. It allows me to play and experiment without an agenda.

There are times when I'm painting in my little studio and hours will go by. I'll be thinking a lot, listening to what God is telling me in my heart. Sometimes I listen to music, but most times it's just me and my art tools hanging out quietly. Very often, I leave my studio feeling lighter as if I just had a nice long talk with an old friend. And you know what? That's what creative time with God can be like.

If you haven't tapped into your creative gifts yet, ask God to just show you the way. Eventually, you'll find your groove. Maybe it will be in sewing, cooking, or just organizing a group of people together. Creativity exists in a lot of places, and you'll know you've found your particular gifts when you feel connected to God.

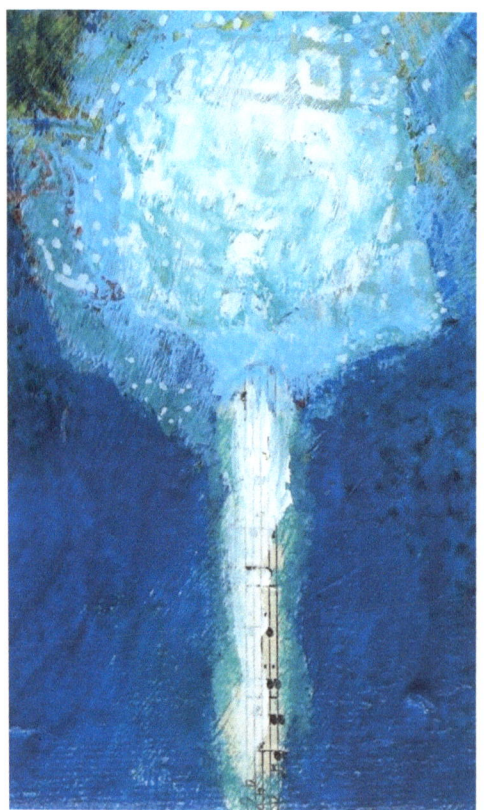

Cherie Burbach

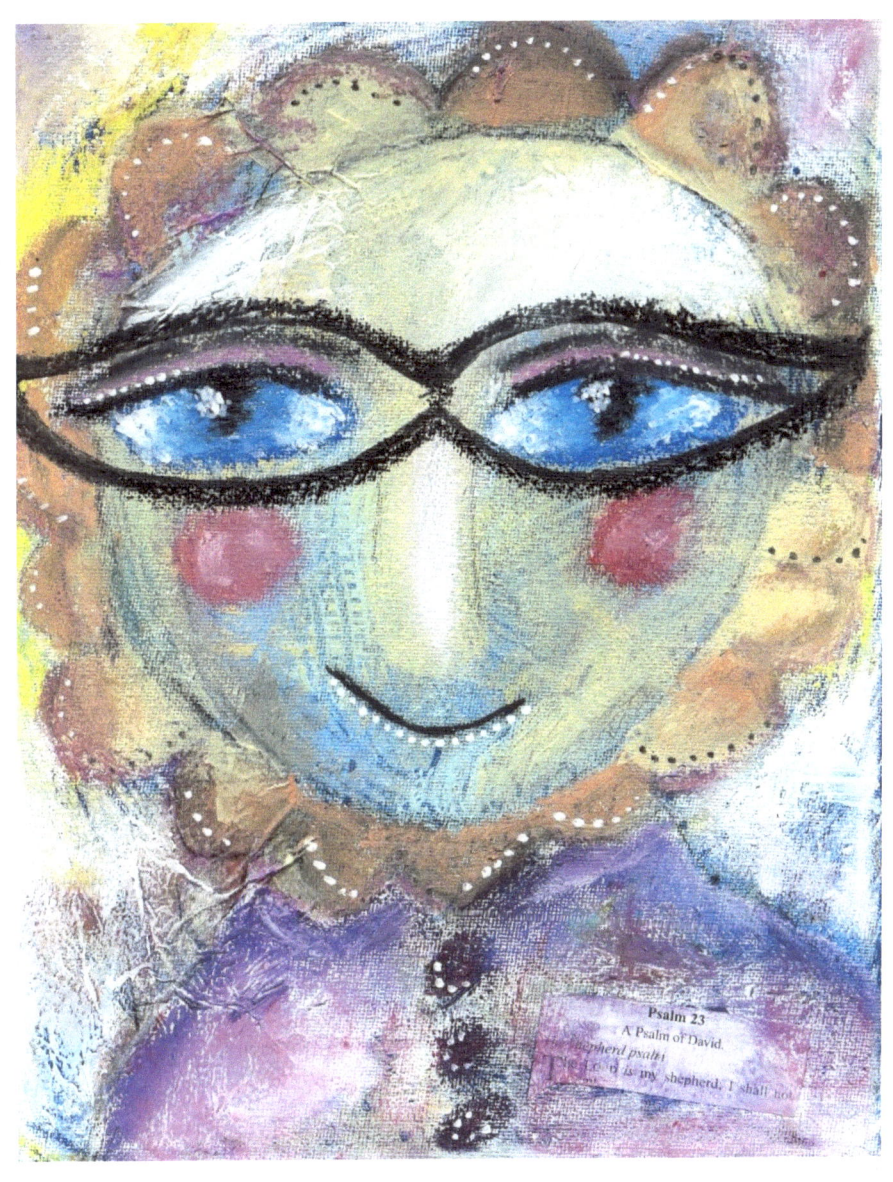

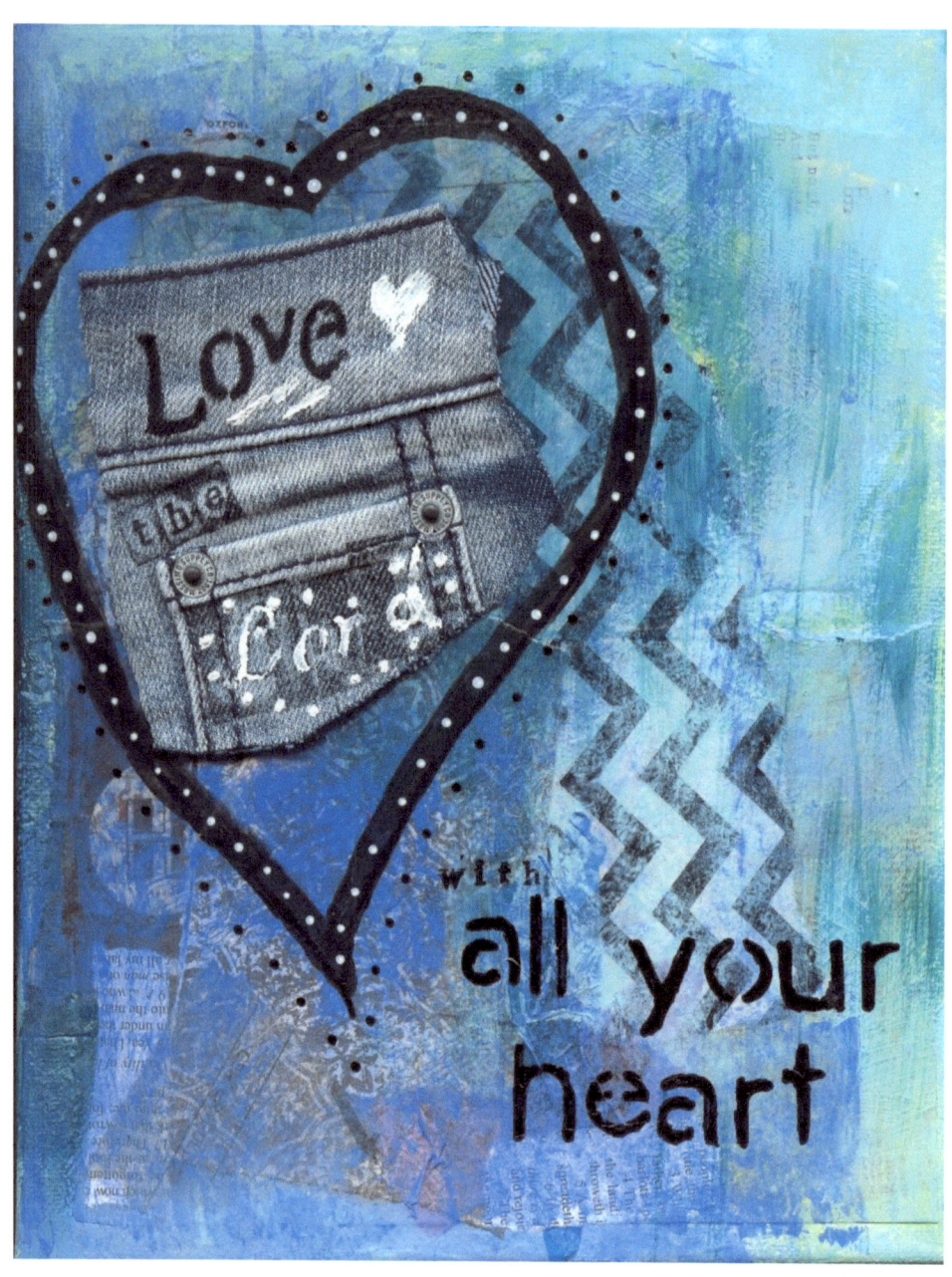

Cherie Burbach

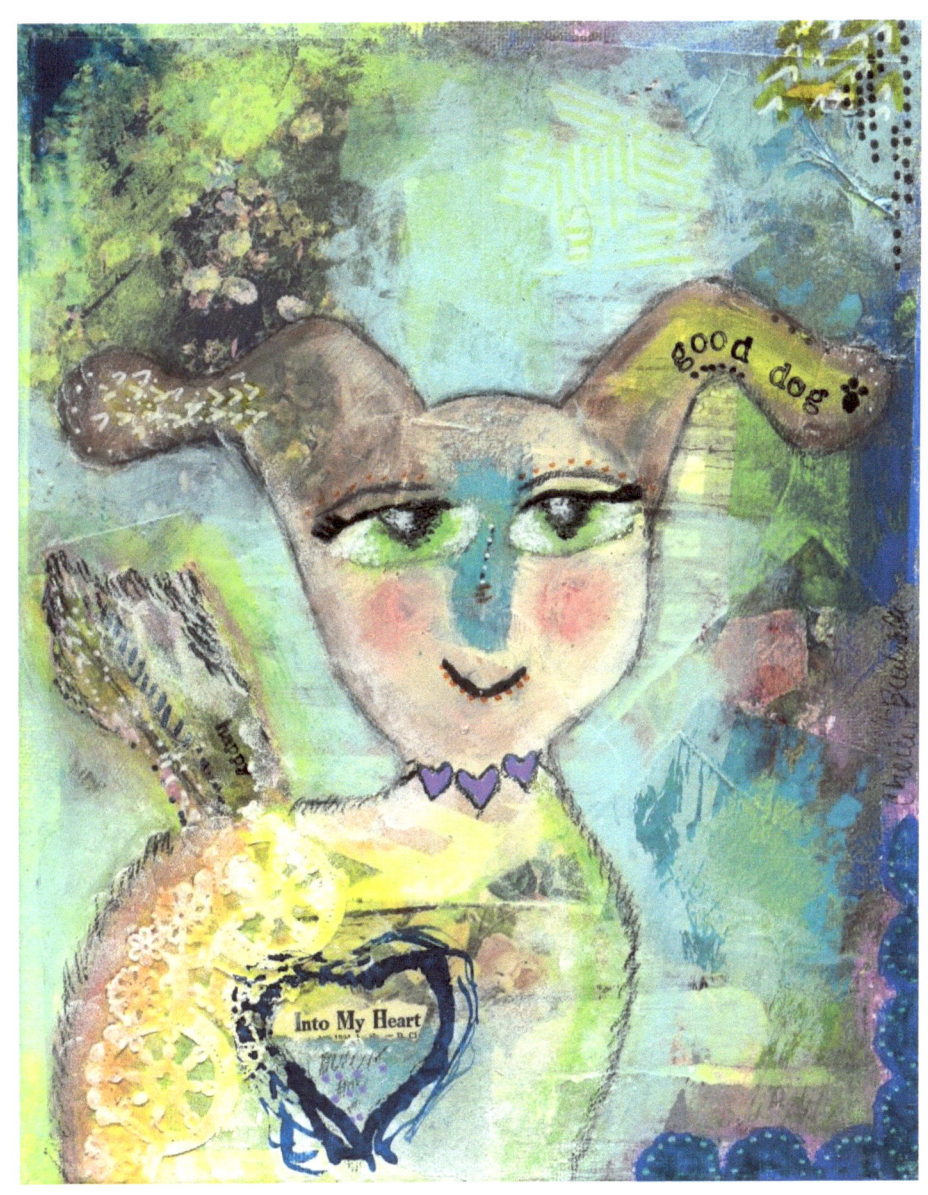

About the Artist

Cherie Burbach specializes in relationships and helping people to connect. Whether it's writing articles or creating art, all of Cherie's work centers on relationships and faith.

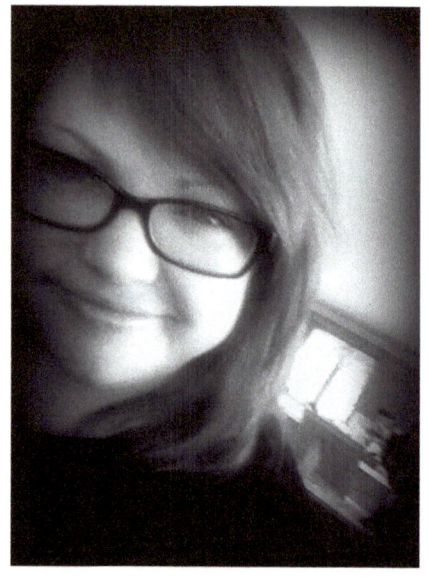

Cherie also likes to express herself with mixed media art, combining Bible verses and her own poetry with special papers and acrylics.

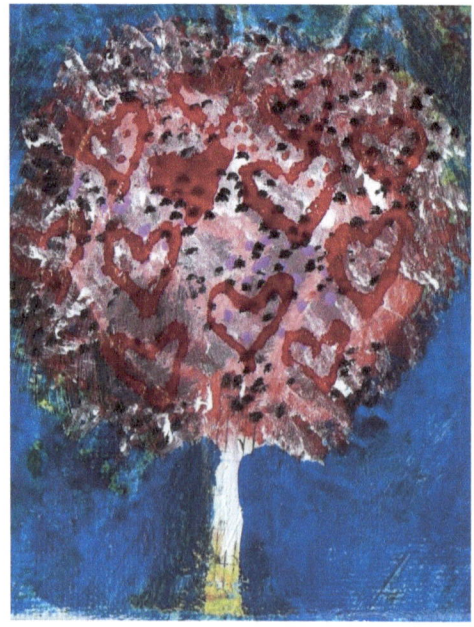

She includes book pages, music sheets, and other fabulous random things in her art to create something that celebrates a hopeful, faith-filled message. You can see some of her works at her Etsy shop and on her website.

Cherie Burbach

Cherie is also a freelance writer and author. She has written for NBC/Universal, Match.com, *Christianity Today*, and more. Cherie's poetry reflects the faith and hope that is evident in her life story. Her nonfiction books help people connect, meet new people, and find balance in their lives.

Learn more about her at: cherieburbach.com.

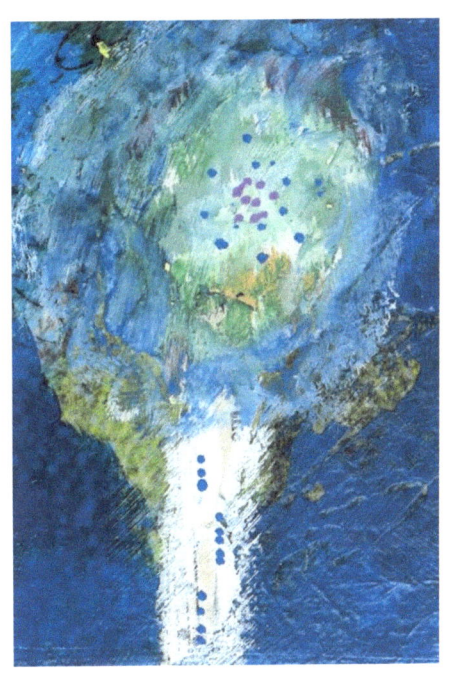

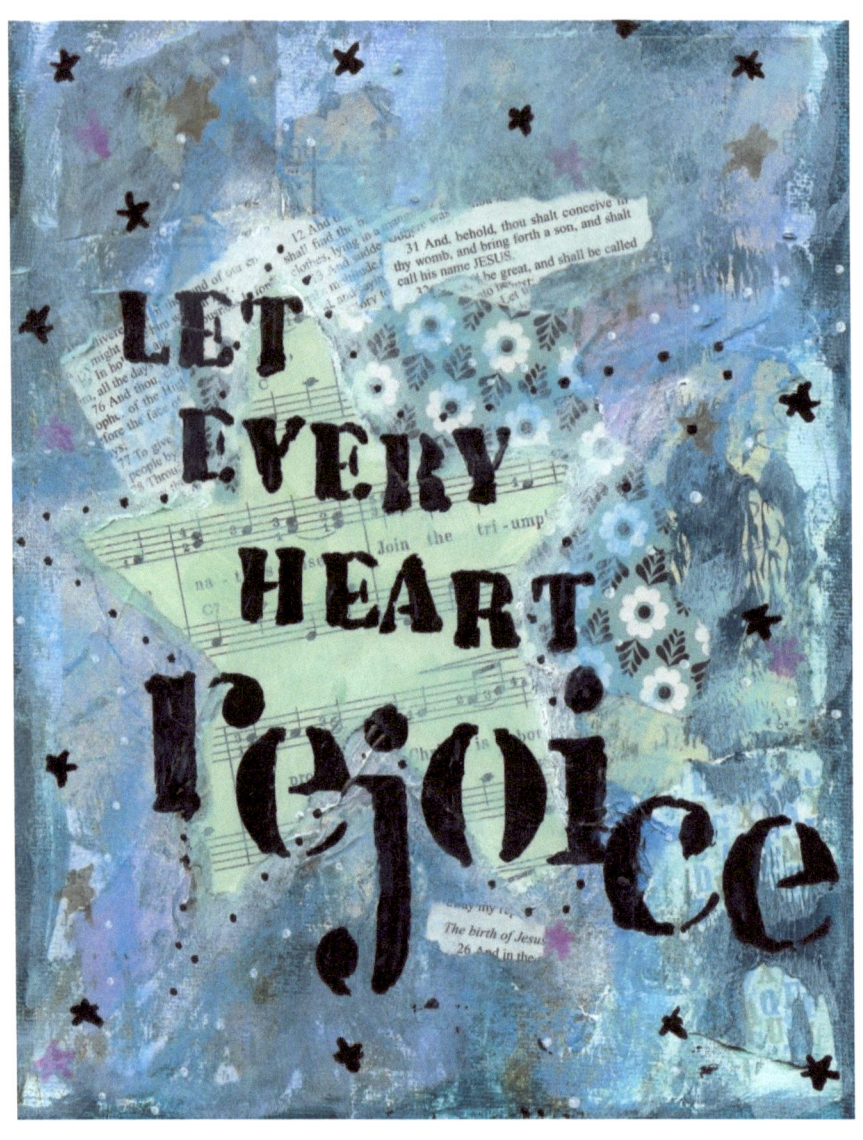

Cherie Burbach

www.ingramcontent.com/pod-product-compliance
Lightning Source LLC
Chambersburg PA
CBHW050852180526
45159CB00007B/2650

* 9 7 8 0 9 9 7 2 2 7 4 0 6 *